EDWIN R. A. SELIGMAN

THE ECONOMIC INTERPRETATION OF HISTORY

Elibron Classics
www.elibron.com

Elibron Classics series.

ISBN 0-543-95195-2 (paperback)
ISBN 0-543-95194-4 (hardcover)

This Elibron Classics Replica Edition is an unabridged facsimile of the edition published in 1907 by the Columbia University Press, New York.

THE
ECONOMIC INTERPRETATION
OF HISTORY

OTHER WORKS BY THE SAME AUTHOR

PRINCIPLES OF ECONOMICS. Third edition. 1907. Longmans, Green & Co.

ESSAYS IN TAXATION. Fifth edition. 1905. The Macmillan Company.

THE SHIFTING AND INCIDENCE OF TAXATION. Second edition. 1899. Columbia University Press.

PROGRESSIVE TAXATION. The Macmillan Company. 1894.

THE ECONOMIC INTERPRETATION OF HISTORY

BY

EDWIN R. A. SELIGMAN

McVICKAR PROFESSOR OF POLITICAL ECONOMY
COLUMBIA UNIVERSITY, NEW YORK

SECOND EDITION, REVISED

New York
THE COLUMBIA UNIVERSITY PRESS
1907

Set up and electrotyped June, 1902.
Second Edition, June, 1907.
Japanese Translation, 1905. Russian Translation, 1906.
Spanish Translation, 1907.

Norwood Press
J. S. Cushing & Co. — Berwick & Smith Co.
Norwood, Mass., U.S.A.

PREFATORY NOTE

THE present work is substantially a reproduction, with some alterations, additions and rearrangements, of the articles that appeared in Volumes XVI and XVII of the *Political Science Quarterly*. The requests for reprints were so numerous that it seemed best to meet the demand by giving to the essays a more permanent form. May the treatment of the subject in the following pages lead to the fuller discussion which so important a topic deserves at the hands of economists, historians and philosophers alike.

COLUMBIA UNIVERSITY.
NEW YORK, May, 1902.

CONTENTS

INTRODUCTION

PART I

HISTORY OF THE THEORY OF ECONOMIC INTERPRETATION

CHAPTER I

CHAPTER II

CHAPTER III

CHAPTER IV

CHAPTER V

CHAPTER VI

PART II

CRITICISM OF THE THEORY OF ECONOMIC INTERPRETATION

CHAPTER I

CHAPTER II

INTRODUCTION

STATEMENT OF THE THESIS

To the student of the social sciences it is interesting to observe the process by which, in one respect at least, we are drifting back to the position of bygone ages. Although Aristotle pointed out the essential interrelation of politics, ethics and economics, modern thought has successfully vindicated the claims of these disciplines, as well as of others, such as jurisprudence and the various divisions of public law, to be considered separate sciences. For a long time, however, to the common detriment of all, the independence of each was so emphasized and exaggerated as to create the serious danger of forgetting that they are only constituent parts of a larger whole. The tendency of recent thought has been to accentuate the relations rather than the differences, and to explain the social institutions which form the bases of the separate sciences in the light rather of a synthesis than of an analysis. This method has been applied to the record of the past, as well as to the facts of the present; the conception of history has been broadened until it is now well recognized that political history is only one phase of that wider activity which includes all the phenomena of social life. If the term "politics" is used in the common but narrow sense of constitutional and diplomatic relations, then to repeat the familiar dictum, "History is past politics," is to utter a half-truth, in lamentable disregard of these newer ideas.

While, however, it is now conceded that the history of mankind is the history of man in society, and therefore social history in its broadest sense, the question has arisen as to the fundamental causes of this social development — the reason of these great changes in human thought and human life which form the conditions of progress. No more profound and far-reaching question can occupy our attention; for upon the correct answer depends our whole attitude toward life itself. It is the supreme problem not only to the scientist, but to the practical man as well. Of this problem one solution has been offered which during the past few decades has been engaging the lively attention of thinkers not alone in Germany, where the theory originated, but in Italy, Russia and, to some extent, in England and France. The echoes of the controversy have scarcely reached our shores; but a movement of thought at once so bold and so profound cannot fail to spread to the uttermost limits of scientific thought and to evoke a discussion adequate to the nature of the problem and the character of the solution.

We may state the thesis succinctly as follows: The existence of man depends upon his ability to sustain himself; the economic life is therefore the fundamental condition of all life. Since human life, however, is the life of man in society, individual existence moves within the framework of the social structure and is modified by it. What the conditions of maintenance are to the individual, the similar relations of production and consumption are to the community. To economic causes, therefore, must be traced in last instance those transformations in the structure of society which themselves condition the relations of social classes and the various manifestations of social life.

This doctrine is often called "historical materialism," or the "materialistic interpretation of history." Such terms are, however, lacking in precision. If by materialism is meant the tracing of all changes to material causes, the biological view of history is also materialistic. Again, the theory which ascribes all changes in society to the influence of climate or to the character of the fauna and flora is materialistic, and yet has little in common with the doctrine here discussed. The doctrine we have to deal with is not only materialistic, but also economic in character; and the better phrase is not the "materialistic interpretation," but the "economic interpretation" of history. In France it has become the fashion to call the theory "economic determinism"; but this is still more objectionable for the reason that it begs the question as to whether there is anything really "deterministic" or fatalistic about the doctrine. This point will be fully discussed hereafter.[1]

In the following pages an attempt will be made to explain the genesis and development of the doctrine, to study some of the applications made by recent thinkers, to examine the objections that may be advanced and, finally, to estimate the true import and value of the theory for modern science.

[1] See part ii, chapter i.

PART I

HISTORY OF THE THEORY OF ECONOMIC INTERPRETATION

CHAPTER I

THE EARLY PHILOSOPHY OF HISTORY

FEW of the leading writers of the eighteenth or the first half of the nineteenth century devoted much attention to the problem of historical causation. The historians were for the most part content to describe the facts of political and diplomatic history; and, when they sought for anything more than the most obvious explanation of the facts, they generally took recourse to the "great man" theory or to the vague doctrine of the "genius of the age." Even the Nestor of modern historical writing, Ranke, attempted scarcely more than to unravel the tangled skein of international complications by showing the influence of foreign politics upon national growth.

While most of the historians gave evidence of only a slight philosophical equipment, the philosophers presented a "philosophy of history" which sometimes showed scarcely more familiarity with history. That Rousseau was not a profound historical scholar, is to put it mildly. Others, like Lessing in his *Education of Humanity*[1] and Herder in his *Ideas on the Philosophy of History*,[2] were too much under the domination of the theistic conception to give much impetus to a newer movement of thought, even though Herder in Germany, like Ferguson[3] in Scotland, may be called in some respects a forerunner of modern anthropological investigations. Huxley, as well as many of the German writers,[4] has pointed out that Kant in his *Idea of a Universal History*[5] anticipated some of the modern doctrines as to the evolution of society; but even Kant was not sufficiently emancipated from the theology of the age to take a strictly scientific view of the subject. With Hegel's *Philosophy of History* we reach the high-water mark of the "idealistic" interpretation; but the Hegelian conception of the "spirit of history" has shown itself at once too subtle and too jejune for general acceptance.

A second but less comprehensive attempt to

[1] *Die Erziehung des Menschengeschlechts.*

[2] *Ideen zur Philosophie der Geschichte der Menschheit.*

[3] *Essay on the History of Civil Society* (1767).

[4] Woltmann, *Der Historische Materialismus* (1900), pp. 17–21.

[5] *Idee zu einer Allgemeinen Geschichte in Weltbürgerlicher Absicht* (1784).

interpret historical growth in terms of thought and feeling was made by those who maintained that religion is the keynote of progress. That each of the five great religions has exerted a profound influence on human development is indubitable—Judaism typifying the idea of duty; Confucianism, of order; Mohammedanism, of justice; Buddhism, of patience; and Christianity, of love. But, entirely apart from the fact that this explanation overlooks the possibility of regarding religion as a product rather than a cause, no light is thrown on the question why the retention of the same religion is often compatible with the most radical changes in the character and condition of its devotees. The religious interpretation of history, even in the modified form of Mr. Benjamin Kidd's theory, has found but few adherents.

A third explanation, which can be traced to Aristotle and which has met with some favor among publicists, might be called the political interpretation of history. It holds, substantially, that throughout all history there can be discerned a definite movement from monarchy to aristocracy, from aristocracy to democracy, and that there is a constant progress from absolutism to freedom, both in idea and in institution. But very many philosophers, including Aristotle himself, have pointed out that democracy might lead to tyranny; and modern anthropology has tended to discredit the existence of the first alleged step. Above all, it has been repeatedly shown that political change is not a primary, but a secondary, phenomenon; and that to erect into a universal cause what is itself a result is to put the cart before the horse.

With the failure of all these attempts of a more or less idealistic nature, the way was prepared for an interpretation of history which would look to physical, rather than to psychical, forces; or rather, which would explain how the psychical forces, into which all social movement may be analyzed, are themselves conditioned by the physical environment. The name with which this doctrine is associated is that of Buckle.

The theory of the predominant influence of the external world on human affairs can be traced to many writers of the eighteenth century, of whom Vico[1] and Montesquieu[2] are

[1] In his *Principii di una Scienza Nuova d' intorno alla Comune Natura delle Nazioni* (1725). As to Vico, see Huth, *Life of Buckle*, I, pp. 233 *et seq.* Buckle says of Vico that, "though his *Scienza Nuova* contains the most profound views on ancient history, they are glimpses of truth rather than a systematic investigation of any one period."

[2] In his *Esprit des Lois*.

easily the most famous.[1] Buckle himself had no small opinion of Montesquieu's merits. He tells us[2] that Montesquieu "knew what no historian before him had even suspected, that in the great march of human affairs, individual peculiarities count for nothing. . . . He effected a complete separation between biography and history, and taught historians to study, not the peculiarities of individual character, but the general aspect of the society in which the peculiarities appeared." Furthermore, we are told, Montesquieu "was the first who, in an inquiry into the relations between the social condition of a country and its jurisprudence, called in the aid of physical knowledge in order to ascertain how the character of any given civilization is modified by the action of the external world."

What Montesquieu, however, stated aphoristically and on the basis of the imperfect physical science of the day, Buckle first worked out philosophically and with such wealth of illustration that he is properly regarded as the

[1] In a complete catalogue of writers who in some way influenced Buckle there ought to be included not only Holbach, Helvetius and Cabanis, but for the early period Bodin, with his theory of climates, and still farther back even Aristotle.

[2] *History of Civilization in England*, 1857, pt. ii, ch. vi (pp. 316–317 of edition of 1873).

real creator of the doctrine. In his celebrated second chapter, entitled "The Influence of Physical Laws," Buckle analyzed the effects of climate, food and soil upon social improvement and its basis, the accumulation of wealth.

Buckle, it is true, as we have been lately reminded,[1] does not claim that all history is to be interpreted in the light of external causes alone. He does, indeed, tell us that in early society the history of wealth depends entirely on soil and climate; but he is careful to add that in a more advanced state of society there are other circumstances which possess an equal, and sometimes a superior, influence.[2] In fact, in a later chapter he maintains that "the advance of European civilization is characterized by a diminishing influence of physical laws and an increasing influence of mental laws"; and he concludes that if, as he has shown, "the measure of civilization is the triumph of the mind over external agents, it becomes clear that of the two classes of laws which regulate the progress of mankind, the mental class is more important than the physical."[3] At the end of

[1] By Robertson, *Buckle and his Critics* (1895).
[2] *History of Civilization*, I, p. 44.
[3] *Ibid.*, pp. 156, 157.

his general analysis he even goes so far as to maintain that "we have found reason to believe that the growth of European civilization is solely due to the progress of knowledge, and that the progress of knowledge depends on the number of truths which the human intellect discovers, and on the extent to which they are diffused."[1]

While it is clear, therefore, that Buckle was by no means so extreme as some of his critics would have us believe, it is none the less probable that his name will remain associated with the doctrine of physical environment. For it was he, after all, who most forcibly and eloquently called attention to the importance of the physical factors and to the influence that they have exerted in moulding national character and social life. Since his time much more has been done, not only in studying, as Buckle himself did, the immediate influence of climate and soil,[2] but also in explaining the allied field of the effect of the fauna and the flora on social development. The subject of the domestication of animals, for instance, and its profound

[1] *History of Civilization*, I, p. 288.

[2] One of the best known, but most uncritical, representatives of this school is Grant Allen, especially in his article "Nation Making" in the *Gentleman's Magazine*, 1873, reprinted in the *Popular Science Monthly* of the same year.

effect on human progress has not only been investigated by a number of recent students,[1] but has been made the very basis of the explanation of early American civilization by one of the most brilliant and most learned of recent historians.[2] A Russian scholar[3] has shown in detail the connection between the great rivers and the progress of humanity, and the whole modern study of economic geography is but an expansion on broader lines of the same idea.

Buckle, however, devoted most of his attention to the influence of physical forces on the production of the food supply. With the difficulties of the problem of distribution, which he confesses are of greater importance, he declares himself unable to grapple. An exception, indeed, is to be made in the case of "a very early stage of society," where Buckle thinks he can prove that "the distribution of wealth is, like its creation, governed entirely by physical laws."[4]

[1] Especially E. Hahn, *Die Hausthiere und ihre Beziehung zur Wirtschaft des Menschen* (1896).

[2] Payne, *History of the New World called America*; especially vol. i, bk. ii. All this was, however, substantially pointed out by Morgan twenty years earlier in his *Ancient Society*, p. 24. For Morgan, see chapter vi, below.

[3] Metchnikoff, *La Civilisation et les Grandes Fleuves Historiques*. Préface d'Elisée Reclus. Paris, 1889.

[4] *Civilization in England*, I, p.52.

His suggestive, but not very successful, attempt to prove this point, which rests upon an acceptance of the one fundamental error of the classical economists — the wages-fund doctrine — can here only be mentioned.[1] It is, however, important to emphasize the fact that, with this one exception, Buckle makes no endeavor to throw any light on the connection between physical environment and the distribution of wealth; for distribution, he tells us, depends on "circumstances of great complexity, which it is not necessary here to examine," and of which, as he adds in a note, "many are still unknown."[2]

[1] Briefly put, the argument is as follows: The two great constituents of food are carbon and oxygen; the colder the country, the more highly carbonized must be the food; nitrogenous foods are less costly than carbonaceous ones. Wages depend on population, population on the food supply; hence the tendency for wages in hot countries is to be low, in cold countries to be high. Finally, wages and profits vary in inverse proportions; or, as he puts it elsewhere, if rent and interest are high, wages are low. Hence the great differentiation of rural classes in hot countries.

[2] *Civilization in England*, I, p. 51. It is amusing to note that the only law which Buckle himself accepts — "the great law of the ratio between the cost of labor and the profits of stock" — is precisely the one which, in its original form, has been discredited by modern economic research. Notwithstanding this fact, Mr. Robertson is so loyal to his hero that he calls it "one of those generalisations by which Buckle really illuminates history." — Robertson, *Buckle and his Critics*, p. 49.

CHAPTER II

PHILOSOPHICAL ANTECEDENTS OF THE THEORY

THE explanation which Buckle made no attempt to give had been advanced more than a decade before by another writer who was destined to become far more famous and influential. Karl Marx enjoyed some qualifications for the task which were denied to Buckle. Buckle was, indeed, well abreast of the foreign, as well as the English, literature on history and natural science; but his economic views were almost entirely in accord with those of the prevalent English school. These principles so completely lacked the evolutionary point of view as to preclude any historical treatment of society. Karl Marx, on the other hand, not only possessed the philosophical and scientific equipment of a German university graduate, but found himself in direct and unqualified opposition to the teachings of the professional economists. While Buckle contented himself with pointing out how physical forces affect the production of wealth, Marx addressed himself to the larger task of showing how the whole structure of society is modified by the relations of social classes, and how these relations are themselves dependent on antecedent economic changes. In Buckle it was primarily the physicist that created a certain materialistic interpretation of history; in Marx it was the socialist that brought about a very different and specifically economic interpretation of history. In order to understand the genesis of the economic interpretation of history it will be necessary to say a few words about the philosophical antecedents of Marx.

Like most of the young Germans of the thirties, Marx was a firm believer in Hegel. The Hegelian philosophy, however, really contained two separate parts, — the dialectical method and the system. The fundamental conception of the Hegelian dialectic is that of process, or development by the union of opposites — a method that advances from notion to notion through negation. In all logic we begin with a half truth; we proceed to its opposite, which is equally false; and we then combine them into a third, which shows that they are equally true, when considered as necessary constituents of the whole.[1] This idea of process, or development, Hegel applied to his celebrated statement: "All that is real is reasonable; all that is reasonable is real." Interpreted in one way, this would mean fatalism, or optimistic conservatism. But according to Hegel everything that exists is by no means real. Only that is real which in the course of its development shows itself to be necessary. When it is no longer necessary, it loses its reality. As some of his followers pointed out, the French government had become so unnecessary by 1789 that not it, but the Revolution, was real. Hence the original statement turns into the opposite: All that is real becomes in the course of time unreasonable, and is thus from the very outset unreal; all that is reasonable in idea is destined to be realized, even though it may for the moment be utterly unreal. The original statements of the reasonableness of what is real, and of the reality of what is reasonable, blend into the higher statement that all that exists is destined some day to pass out of existence.[2]

[1] Bonar, *Philosophy and Political Economy*, p. 300; and Schwegler, *History of Philosophy*, translated by Stirling (5th ed., 1875), p. 324.

[2] F. Engels, *Ludwig Feuerbach und der Ausgang der Klassischen Deutschen Philosophie*, 1888 (2d ed., 1895), p. 3.

The importance of this dialectical method lay in the idea of process — in the realization of the fact that the conclusions of human thought and action are not final. Translated into social and political language, it formed the basis of the aspirations of the liberal and progressive elements in the community. On the other hand, Hegel himself never drew these radical conclusions from his theory because, although in his logic he made it clear that the truth is nothing but the dialectical process itself, he nevertheless posited, as a result of his whole philosophy, the conception of the "absolute idea." Into the mysteries of this absolute idea we are not called upon to penetrate; it is sufficient to point out that, as applied to the domain of social politics, it results in a moderate conservatism. It is in the then existing German state that, according to Hegel, universality and individuality, law and liberty — the highest stage of the universal spirit — find their reconciliation!

The antagonism between the dialectical and the absolute system of Hegel was not at first perceived. Just as both individualists and socialists to-day claim Adam Smith as the fountain head of their doctrines, so for a time both radicals and conservatives in Germany harked back to Hegel. Toward the end of the thirties the schism became apparent. The Young-Hegelians swore by the dialectical method and landed in radicalism; the orthodox followers remained true to the "absolute idea" and became reactionaries. At first, however, politics was a dangerous field to enter, and the discussion turned on religion. As either Catholicism or Evangelical Protestantism was the state religion in each of the German states, the attack on religion was indirectly political in character, and was recognized as such.

Strauss had set the ball rolling in 1835 by his *Life of Jesus*. His assertion of the mythical character of the evangelist accounts led to a famous dispute with Bruno Bauer, who went one step farther and maintained that they were not even myths, but pure fabrications. In this reaction against the foundations of the state religion the Young-Hegelians were practically forced back to the philosophical materialism of England and France in the eighteenth century. But they now recognized the antagonism between their new views and the doctrine of Hegel. While the philosophical materialists had posited nature as the only reality, Hegel regarded the absolute idea — that is, the intellect and its logical process — as the fundamental conception, and nature as only the derivative or the reflex of the absolute idea.

The uncertainty continued until the early forties, when Feuerbach published his *Essence of Christianity*,[1] in which he sought to demolish the idealistic or transcendental basis of all theology. In this work Feuerbach claimed that nature exists independently of philosophy, that there is in reality nothing but nature and man, and that our religious conceptions are a product of ourselves, who again are nothing but a product of nature. Who has not heard of Feuerbach's famous phrase: *Der Mensch ist was er isst* — "Man is what he eats"? Feuerbach at once showed the Young-Hegelians that, important as the Hegelian dialectics may have been, the "absolute idea" was not the basis, but the product.

Feuerbach exerted a profound influence on the thinkers of the day. Curiously enough, however, he also, in the domain of social politics, gave rise to two antagonistic schools. Although in his philosophy a materialist, or rather a "naturalist," there was a decidedly

[1] *Das Wesen des Christenthums.*

idealistic strain in his ethical doctrine. With him religion is what the etymology of the word implies, — the really important thing that binds men together. Of his attempt to erect an idealistic religion on a naturalistic basis, this is not the place to speak.[1] But it is important to point out that his doctrine of love as the basis of all religion led to the so-called "true" or "philosophical" socialism of the forties in Germany. The early socialists had accepted the views of the French reformers, St. Simon and Fourier. Now they asserted that all that was necessary was to apply Feuerbach's "humanism" to social relations, in order to proclaim the speedy regeneration of mankind. The leaders of the "philosophical" socialists, Karl Grün and Moses Hess,[2] for a time dominated the social movement in Germany.

While the superimposed idealism of Feuerbach led to the "philosophical socialism" of the forties, his original and basic naturalism helped to produce in Karl Marx the founder of "scientific socialism." Marx was educated in Hegel-

[1] *Cf.* Lange, *Geschichte des Materialismus*, vol. ii (3d ed., 1877), pp. 73–81.

[2] For their views in detail, see George Adler, *Die Geschichte der ersten Sozial-politischen Arbeiterbewegung in Deutschland*, pp. 83–85.

ianism, and to the end of his days loved to coquet with the Hegelian dialectic. He had become a Young-Hegelian and was deeply influenced by the appearance of Feuerbach's book. This set him thinking. The materialistic idea he accepted as beyond dispute, but he recognized some of its weaknesses. The materialism of the eighteenth century was essentially mechanical and unhistorical. It had developed before science had assumed its modern garb. The watchword of modern science is that of evolution through natural selection.

Although this had not yet been proclaimed even by the natural scientists, or at all events had certainly not been applied by any one to social conceptions, the idea was in the air; and, although Marx was not at first specially well versed in natural science, the naturalism of Feuerbach, combined with the conception of process in the dialectic of Hegel, led him finally to the theory that all social institutions are the result of a growth, and that the causes of this growth are to be sought not in any idea, but in the conditions of material existence. In other words, it led him to the economic interpretation of history. He then broke at once with the philosophical or sentimental socialists, and devoted all his time henceforth to the deeper study of economic conditions.

That Marx's analysis of economic conditions led him to scientific socialism is a thing by itself, with which we have here no concern; for that is an economic theory, based upon his doctrines of surplus value and profits, which have been engaging the attention of economists throughout the world. We need to lay stress on Marx's philosophy, rather than on his economics; and his philosophy, as we now know, resulted in his economic interpretation of history. It chanced that he also became a socialist; but his socialism and his philosophy of history are, as we shall see later, really independent. One can be an "economic materialist" and yet remain an extreme individualist. The fact that Marx's economics may be defective has no bearing on the truth or falsity of his philosophy of history.

CHAPTER III

GENESIS AND DEVELOPMENT OF THE THEORY

LET us now proceed to illustrate the development of the new doctrine from the writings of Marx himself. It will be advisable to quote freely, because these earlier works of Marx are little known even in Germany, and are almost unknown outside of Germany.[1] Yet they are of the utmost importance in showing the genesis of an idea which is now one of the storm centres not only of economic and social, but also of philosophical, discussion.

In his earliest essays we see only the radical political reformer. As a young man of twenty-four, he was called in 1842 to the editorship of the *Rheinische Zeitung*, a daily paper started

[1] Just as these lines go to the printer, an announcement is made of the impending publication, in three volumes, of the more important of Marx's essays between 1841 and 1850, under the title: *Aus dem Literarischen Nachlass von Karl Marx, Friedrich Engels und Ferdinand Lassalle. Herausgegeben von Franz Mehring. Gesammelte Schriften von Karl Marx und Friedrich Engels, 1841 bis 1850.* Erster Band: Von März, 1841, bis März, 1844. Stuttgart, Dietz, 1901–1902.

in Cologne by some of the Young-Hegelians who belonged to the radical party. While battling for political reforms Marx had his attention called for the first time to economic questions. He severely criticised the historical school of jurisconsults, because they regarded all existing legal institutions as the necessary, and therefore the wise, result of a long evolution. To their optimistic conservatism Marx opposed the Hegelian idea of liberty.

It was not, however, until after the *Rheinische Zeitung* had been suspended by the government in 1843 that Marx went to Paris [1] and became a socialist — influenced largely by St. Simon and Proudhon, and possibly by the celebrated book of Lorenz Stein, which appeared the year before, on the socialistic and communistic movement in France.[2] At Paris, Marx started in 1844, in conjunction with another leader of the

[1] In the mean time he published anonymously a violent article on the Prussian censorship, in the *Anekdota zur Neuesten Deutschen Philosophie und Publicistik*, von Bruno Bauer, Ludwig Feuerbach, Friedrich Köppen, Karl Nauwerk, Arnold Ruge und einigen Ungenannten, 1843. One of these "Ungenannten" was Karl Marx, who wrote under the title of a "Rhinelander." The article may be found in vol. i, pp. 56–88.

[2] It is more than probable, however, that Marx was converted to socialism wholly by the French writers, who themselves exerted so great an influence on Stein. *Cf.* the correspondence of Arnold Ruge, vol. i.

Young-Hegelians, Arnold Ruge, the *Deutsch-Französische Jahrbücher*. Here the beginning of the opposition to the French communists is perceptible; for in the introductory editorial we are told that what has saved Germany from "the metaphysical and fantastical ideas of Lamennais, Proudhon, St. Simon and Fourier" is the Hegelian logic.[1] Yet Marx showed the influence of Feuerbach by writing an article in criticism of Hegel's *Philosophy of Law*, in which he sought to prove how theological criticism was now necessarily being replaced by political criticism.

Marx, indeed, went a step farther, and emphasized the necessity of a revolution of the fourth estate, — the proletariat. He was beginning to formulate his ideas on economic questions. "The relation of industry and of the world of wealth in general to the political world is the chief problem of modern times."[2] In another place he tells us that "revolutions

[1] *Deutsch-Französische Jahrbücher. Herausgegeben von Arnold Ruge und Karl Marx.* Erste und Zweite Lieferung, 1844, p. 8. *Cf.* also: "Uns Deutsche hat . . . von der Willkür und Phantastik das Hegelsche System befreit."

[2] "Das Verhältniss der Industrie, überhaupt der Welt des Reichthums zu der politischen Welt ist ein Hauptproblem der modernen Zeit." — *Ibid.*, p. 75.

need a passive element, a material basis."[1] In a later essay in the same periodical on the "Jewish Question," in which he opposed the views of Bruno Bauer, Marx claims that "we must emancipate ourselves before we can emancipate others."[2] He seeks to show that the importance of the French Revolution consisted in freeing not only the political forces of society, but also the economic basis on which the political superstructure rested.[3] The political change was in a certain sense idealism; but it marked at the same time the materialism of society.[4]

The double number of the *Deutsch-Französische Jahrbücher* was the only one that appeared. Ruge and Marx could not agree in their attitude toward the question of communism. While in Paris, however, Marx formed

[1] "Die Revolutionen bedürfen nämlich eines passiven Elementes, einer materiellen Grundlage. . . . Die Theorie wird in einem Volke immer nur so weit verwircklicht als sie die Verwircklichung seiner Bedürfnisse ist." — *Deutsch-Französische Jahrbücher*, p. 80.

[2] *Ibid.*, p. 184.

[3] "Die politische Emancipation ist zugleich die Auflösung der alten Gesellschaft, auf welcher das dem Volk entfremdete Staatswesen, die Herrschermacht, ruht. Die politische Revolution ist die Revolution der bürgerlichen Gesellschaft." — *Ibid.*, p. 204.

[4] "Allein die Vollendung des Idealismus des Staats war zugleich die Vollendung des Materialismus der bürgerlichen Gesellschaft." — *Ibid.*, p. 205.

an intimacy with his lifelong friend, Frederick Engels, whose acquaintance he had originally made while both were working on the editorial staff of the *Rheinische Zeitung*.[1] They now decided to write in common a work against Bruno Bauer, who represented the more speculative wing of the Young-Hegelians. This appeared in 1845 under the title of *The Holy Family*.[2]

In this book, written almost entirely by Marx, he shows the strong influence of Feuerbach.[3] As he was at that time, however, more interested in opposing the transcendental notions of the other Young-Hegelians in general than in emphasizing the differences between himself and the "sentimental" socialists, it will not surprise us to find him defending Proudhon.[4] Yet even here Marx shows the

[1] Some correspondence of this early period is preserved in "Aus den Briefen von Engels an Marx" in *Die Neue Zeit*, XIX (1901), ii, pp. 505 *et seq.*

[2] *Die Heilige Familie oder Kritik der Kritischen Kritik. Gegen Bruno Bauer und Consorten.* Von Friedrich Engels und Karl Marx. Frankfurt a. M., 1845.

[3] *Cf.* the enthusiastic description of Feuerbach on p. 139 and the disdainful attitude toward Hegel on p. 126.

[4] "Proudhon's Schrift 'Qu'est-ce que la Propriété' hat dieselbe Bedeutung für die moderne Nationalökonomie, welche Say's [evidently a misprint for Sieyès'] Schrift 'Qu'est-ce que le tiers État' für die moderne Politik hat." —*Ibid.*, p. 36.

essentially mechanical nature of the older French materialism, and points out how the philosophic materialism of Helvetius and Holbach led to the socialism of Babœuf and Fourier.[1] Incidentally, Marx calls attention to the economic basis of the French Revolution, and points out that the individual of the French Revolution differed from the individual of classic antiquity because his economic and industrial relations were different.[2] Finally, in another passage he asks outright: —

"Do these gentlemen think that they can understand the first word of history as long as they exclude the relations of man to nature, natural science and industry? Do they believe that they can actually comprehend any epoch without grasping the industry of the period, the immediate methods of production in actual

[1] "Fourier geht unmittelbar von der Lehre der französischen Materialisten aus. Die Babouvisten waren rohe uncivilisirte Materialisten, aber auch der entwickelte Communismus datirt direkt von dem französischen Materialismus." — *Op. cit.*, p. 207, and the quotations on pp. 209–211. As the volume is extremely scarce, it may be noted that a part of this chapter was reprinted in *Die Neue Zeit*, III (1885), pp. 385–395.

[2] In speaking of a placard containing the Declaration of Rights, Marx says: "Eben diese Tabelle proklamirte das Recht eines Menschen, der nicht der Mensch des antiken Gemeinwesens sein kann, so wenig als seine nationalökonomischen und industriellen Verhältnisse die antiken sind." — *Ibid.*, p. 192.

life? . . . Just as they separate the soul from the body, and themselves from the world, so they separate history from natural science and industry, so they find the birthplace of history not in the gross material production on earth, but in the misty cloud formation of heaven."[1]

Although we find in Marx's early works only these incidental allusions to the doctrine of economic interpretation, we are told by Engels, the literary executor of Marx, that Marx had worked out his theory by 1845.[2] That Engels

[1] "Oder glaubt die kritische Kritik in der Erkenntniss der geschichtlichen Wirklichkeit auch nur zum Anfang gekommen zu sein, so lange sie das theoretische und praktische Verhältniss des Menschen zur Natur, die Naturwissenschaft und die Industrie, aus der geschichtlichen Bewegung ausschliesst? Oder meint sie irgend eine Periode in der That schon erkannt zu haben, ohne z. B. die Industrie dieser Periode, die unmittelbare Produktionsweise des Lebens selbst, erkannt zu haben? . . . Wie sie das Denken von dem Sinnen, die Seele vom Leibe, sich selbst von der Welt trennt, so trennt sie die Geschichte von der Naturwissenschaft und Industrie, so sieht sie nicht in der grobmateriellen Produktion auf der Erde, sondern in der dunstigen Wolkenbildung am Himmel die Geburtstätte der Geschichte." — *Die Heilige Familie*, p. 238.

[2] "The 'manifesto' being our joint production, I consider myself bound to state that the fundamental proposition which forms its nucleus belongs to Marx. That proposition is: that in every historical epoch the prevailing mode of economic production and exchange, and the social organization necessarily following from it, form the basis upon which it is built up, and from which alone can be explained the political and intellectual history of that epoch; that, consequently, *etc. etc.* . . .

"This proposition, which in my opinion is destined to do for is quite correct in this is shown not only by the quotations just mentioned, but also by the annotations which Marx made to Feuerbach in 1845.[1] Marx here objects to the old mechanical materialistic doctrine that men are simply the results of their environment, because it forgets that this environment can itself be changed by man.[2] He also takes exception to Feuerbach's whole view of religion, on the ground that Feuerbach fails to perceive that man is the product of his social relations and that religion itself is a social outgrowth.[3] A fuller statement

history what Darwin's theory has done for biology, we both had been rapidly approaching for some years before 1845. . . . But when I again met Marx . . . in spring, 1845, he had it already worked out, and put it before me in terms almost as clear as those in which I have stated it here." — *Manifesto of the Communist Party*, by Marx and Engels. Authorized English translation, edited and annotated by Frederick Engels, 1888, preface, pp. 5, 6. This preface was written in English by Engels, and appeared in German only in subsequent editions.

1 Published as an appendix to *Ludwig Feuerbach und der Ausgang der Klassischen Deutschen Philosophie*. Von Friedrich Engels. Mit Anhang, Karl Marx über Feuerbach, vom Jahre 1845 (1888).

2 "Die materialistische Lehre, dass die Menschen Produkte der Umstände und der Erziehung sind, vergisst, dass die Umstände eben von den Menschen verändert werden und dass der Erzieher selbst erzogen werden muss." — *Op. cit.*, p. 80.

3 "Feuerbach löst das religiöse Wesen in das menschliche Wesen auf. Aber das menschliche Wesen ist kein . . . Abstraktum. In seiner Wirklichkeit, ist es das Ensemble der gesellschaftlichen Verhältnisse. . . . Feuerbach sieht nicht, dass das

of his new[1] position, however, is found in some recently discovered essays which were written at about that time.[2] These articles, published anonymously in the *Westfälischer Dampfboot*,[3] are of cardinal importance because Marx now for the first time emphasized his disagreement with the "sentimental socialists."

In the first series of articles, Marx criticises a German communistic sheet published in New York, which was devoting much attention to the Anti-Rent Riots.[4] Marx discusses the agrarian movement in the United States and tries to show from his new point of view the connection be-

'religiöse Gemüth' selbst ein gesellschaftliches Produkt ist."—*Ludwig Feuerbach*, p. 81.

[1] Peter von Struve claims that this new position was not occupied by Marx until 1846. *Cf.* his articles, "Zur Entwicklungsgeschichte des wissenschaftlichen Sozialismus," in *Die Neue Zeit*, XV (1897), i, p. 68, and ii, pp. 228, 269. Struve, however, seems to lay too little stress on the points emphasized above. *Cf.* also the article of Kampffmeyer, "Die ökonomischen Grundlagen des deutschen Sozialismus," in *Die Neue Zeit*, V (1887), especially p. 536, where attention is called to Marx's historical interpretation of history in his letters to Ruge in 1843.

[2] The substance of these essays has been printed by Struve in *Die Neue Zeit*, XIV (1896), 41–48, under the title of "Zwei bisher unbekannte Aufsätze von Karl Marx aus den vierziger Jahren. Ein Beitrag zur Entstehungsgeschichte des wissenschaftlichen Sozialismus."

[3] A monthly review edited by Otto Lüning, which lived from 1845 to 1848.

[4] *Der Volkstribun*, edited by H. Kriege in 1846.

tween economic and political phenomena. In a second series of articles[1] he joins issue with Grün and Hess, the chief advocates of philosophical socialism, and ridicules their failure to perceive that an alteration in methods of production brings about changes in the whole social life.[2]

By 1847[3] Marx had made a somewhat deeper study of economic history. He was now so convinced of the truth of his new theory that he proceeded to make a furious onslaught on

[1] "Karl Grün, die soziale Bewegung in Frankreich und Belgien oder die Geschichtsschreibung des wahren Sozialismus." This appeared early in 1847. The whole of this essay has now been printed, with an introduction by E. Bernstein, in *Die Neue Zeit*, XVIII (1900), pp. 4, 37, 132, 164.

[2] "Herr Grün vergisst, dass Brot heutzutage durch Dampfmühlen, früher durch Wind und Wassermühlen, noch früher durch Handmühlen produzirt wurde, dass diese verschiedenen Produktionsweisen vom blossen Brotessen gänzlich unabhängig sind. . . . Dass mit diesen verschiedenen Stufen der Produktion auch verschiedene Verhältnisse der Produktion zur Consumtion, verschiedene Widersprüche beider gegeben sind, dass diese Widersprüche zu verstehen sind nur aus einer Betrachtung, zu lösen nur durch eine praktische Veränderung, der jedesmeligen Produktionsweise und des gan, en darauf basirenden gesellschaftlichen Zustandes: das ahnt Herr Grün nicht." (*Die Neue Zeit*, XIV, ii, p. 51.) That the difference between Marx and the "true socialists" has often been exaggerated is claimed by Mehring in *Die Neue Zeit*, XIV, ii, p. 401.

[3] In this year Marx also published an article in the *Deutsche Brüsseler Zeitung* entitled "Die moralisierende Kritik und die kritisierende Moral, ein Beitrag zur deutschen Kulturgeschichte." It was directed against Karl Heinzen and was of very much the same character as his attack on Grün.

the older socialists in the person of their chief representative — Proudhon. In reply to Proudhon's *Philosophy of Misery* Marx wrote his *Misery of Philosophy*. Here he elaborates the theory that economic institutions are historical categories and that history itself must be interpreted in the light of economic development. We read — in French, it is true, for Marx wrote equally well in German, English and French — that the conception of private property changes in each historical epoch, in a series of entirely different social relations.[1] In a more general way Marx contends that all social relations are intimately connected with the productive forces of society. He tells us that

"in changing the modes of production, mankind changes all its social relations. The hand mill creates a society with the feudal lord; the steam mill a society with the industrial capitalist. The

1 "A chaque époque historique, la propriété s'est developpée différemment et dans une série de rapports sociaux entièrement différents. Ainsi définir la propriété bourgeoise n'est autre chose que faire l'exposé de tous les rapports sociaux de la production bourgeoise. Vouloir donner une définition de la propriété comme d'un rapport indépendant, d'une catégorie à part, d'une idée abstraite et éternelle, cela ne peut être qu'une illusion de métaphysique ou de jurisprudence." — *Misère de la Philosophie. Réponse à la Philosophie de la Misère de M. Proudhon.* Par Karl Marx, 1847, p. 153.

same men who establish social relations in conformity with their material production also create principles, ideas and categories in conformity with their social relations. . . . All such ideas and categories are therefore historical and transitory products."[1]

In another place he maintains that "the relations in which the productive forces of society manifest themselves, far from being eternal laws, correspond to definite changes in man and in his productive forces."[2] Marx applies this general law in many ways. Thus, in an

[1] "Les rapports sociaux sont intimement liés aux forces productives. En acquirant de nouvelles forces productives les hommes changent leur mode de production, et en changeant leur mode de production, la manière de gagner leur vie, ils changent tous leurs rapports sociaux. Le moulin à bras vous donnera la société avec le suzerain; le moulin à vapeur, la société avec le capitaliste industriel. . . . Les mêmes hommes qui établissent les rapports sociaux conformément à leur productivité matérielle produisent aussi les principes, les idées, les catégories, conformément à leurs rapports sociaux. . . . Ainsi ces idées, ces catégories, sont aussi peu éternelles que les relations qu'elles expriment. Elles sont des produits historiques et transitoires."—*Misère de la Philosophie*, pp. 99, 100.

[2] "N'est-ce pas dire assez que le mode de production, les rapports dans lesquels les forces productives se développent, ne sont rien moins que des lois éternelles, mais qu'ils correspondent à un développement déterminé des hommes et de leurs forces productives, et qu'un changement survenu dans les forces productives des hommes amène nécessairement un changement dans les rapports de production."—*Ibid.*, p. 115; *cf.* pp. 152, 177.

acute study of the doctrine of rent, he points out that rent in the Ricardian sense is nothing but "patriarchal agriculture transformed into commercial industry";[1] and, after explaining the historical growth of modern agricultural conditions, he concludes by objecting to the whole classical school, because it fails to see that economic institutions can be understood only as historical categories.[2] In another passage he contends that money itself is not a thing, but a social relation, and that this relation corresponds to a definite form of production in precisely the same way as exchanges between individuals.[3] Finally, in analyzing the essence of machinery and the historical importance of the principle of division of labor, Marx

[1] "La rente, dans le sens de Ricardo, c'est l'agriculture patriarcale transformée en industrie commerciale, le capital industriel appliqué à la terre, la bourgeoisie des villes transplantée dans les campagnes." — *Misère de la Philosophie*, p. 159.

[2] "Ricardo aprés avoir supposé la production bourgeoise comme nécessaire pour déterminer la rente, l'applique néanmoins à la propriété foncière de toutes les époques et de tous les pays. Ce sont là les errements de tous les économistes qui répresentent les rapports de la production bourgeoise comme des catégories éternelles." — *Ibid.*, p. 160.

[3] "La monnaie, ce n'est pas une chose, c'est un rapport social. . . . Ce rapport est un anneau et comme tel, intimement lié à tout l'enchaînement des autres rapports économiques; . . . ce rapport corréspond à un mode de production determiné, ni plus ni moins que l'échange individuel." — *Ibid.*, p. 64.

tells us that "machinery is not any more of an economic category than is the ox that pulls the plough; it is a productive force. The modern factory, which is itself based on machinery, is a social relation, an economic category."[1] In short, social life at any one time is the result of an economic evolution.

In the famous *Manifesto of the Communist Party*,[2] which appeared the following year, we find the implications, rather than the direct statement, of the principle. After describing how the guild system of industry gave way to the modern industrial system, based on the world market and on the revolution in industrial production, Marx points out that the *bourgeoisie*, in revolutionizing the methods of production, alters with them the whole character of society, and displaces feudalism with modern conditions. At the present day this is a truism; but at the time the manifesto appeared it was a novel and striking conception. Unfortunately, the thought was so inextricably interwoven with

[1] "Les machines ne sont plus une catégorie économique que ne saurait être le bœuf que traîne la charrue. Les machines ne sont qu'une force productive. L'atelier moderne, qui repose sur l'application des machines, est un rapport social de production, une catégorie économique." — *Misère de la Philosophie*, p. 128.

[2] *Manifest der Kommunistischen Partei* (London, 1848), pp. 4–7.

Marx's peculiarly socialistic explanation of the effects of machinery, of the function of capital and of the speedy cataclysm of society, that it created at the time but little impression.

In the succeeding years Marx made various applications of his theory. In 1849 he published a series of articles on *Wage-Labor and Capital*, in the course of which he traced the reason for the change from slavery to serfdom and to the wages system, and again laid down the principle that all relations of society depend upon changes in the economic life and more particularly in the modes of production. He tells us that

"with the change in the social relations by means of which individuals produce, that is, in the social relations of production, and with the alteration and development of the material means of production, the powers of production are also transformed. The relations of production collectively form those social relations which we call society, and a society with definite degrees of historical development. . . . Ancient society, feudal society, bourgeois society, are simply instances of this collective result of the complexes of relations of production, each of which marks an important step in the historical development of mankind."[1]

In a series of articles published in 1850, on "The Class Struggles in France from 1848 to 1850," Marx made the first attempt to apply his principle to an existing political situation.[2] He endeavored to show that the great crisis of 1847 was the real cause of the February revolution, and that the economic reaction of 1849 and 1850 was the basis of the political reaction throughout the Continent. He followed this in 1852 by another article on "The Eighteenth Brumaire," in which he attempted to lay bare the economic foundations of the *coup d'État* in France, and to show that the empire really depended on the small farmer or peasant, who had now become a conservative in place of a revolutionist.[3] It is in this work that we find

[1] "Lohnarbeit und Kapital," *Neue Rheinische Zeitung, Politisch-ökonomische Revue*, redigirt von Karl Marx, April, 1849. This was a series of lectures which Marx delivered in 1847 to a Brussels labor union. They have recently been translated by J. L. Joynes and published in pamphlet form under the title, *Wage-Labor and Capital* (London, 1897).

[2] These articles appeared under the simple title "1848–1849" in the *Neue Rheinische Zeitung*, 1850. They were not published in pamphlet form until 1895, when Engels edited them under the title *Die Klassenkämpfe in Frankreich, 1848 bis 1850.*

[3] "Der Achtzehnte Brumaire des Louis Bonaparte" constituted the second number of a political monthly called *Die Revolution*,

the interesting bit of social psychology in which the ideals of life themselves, as well as the views of any one individual, no matter how eminent, are traced to social and economic causes. Marx informs us that

"on the various forms of property, on the conditions of social existence, there rises an entire superstructure of various and peculiarly formed sensations, illusions, methods of thought and views of life. The whole class fashions and moulds them from out of their material foundations and their corresponding social relations. The single individual, in whom they converge through tradition and education, is apt to imagine that they constitute the real determining causes and the point of departure of his action."[1]

edited in New York in 1852 by Joseph Weydemeyer. It was reprinted as a separate pamphlet by Marx in 1869. A third edition was published in cheap form in 1885.

[1] "Auf den verschiedenen Formen des Eigenthums, auf den sozialen Existenzbedingungen, erhebt sich ein ganzer Ueberbau verschiedener und eigenthümlich gestalteter Empfindungen, Illusionen, Denkweisen und Lebensanschauungen. Die ganze Klasse schafft und gestaltet sie aus ihren materiellen Grundlagen heraus und aus den entsprechenden gesellschaftlichen Verhältnissen. Das einzelne Individuum, dem sie durch Tradition und Erziehung zufliessen, kann sich einbilden, dass sie die eigentlichen Bestimmungsgründe und den Ausgangspunkt seines Handelns bilden." — *Op. cit.*, 2d ed., p. 26.

In another passage he contends that "men make their own history, but they make it not of their own accord or under self-chosen conditions, but under given and transmitted conditions. The tradition of all dead generations weighs like a mountain on the brain of the living."[1]

During the early fifties, largely through the efforts of Mr. Charles A. Dana, Marx was engaged to write a series of articles for the New York *Tribune*, which, under the editorship of Horace Greeley, was devoting considerable attention to the Fourierist socialistic movement in the United States. In these articles,[2] which appeared in English for a period of over eight years, some of them anonymously, as editorials of the *Tribune*, Marx discussed the general

[1] "Die Menschen machen ihr eigene Geschichte, aber sie machen sie nicht aus freien Stücken, nicht unter selbstgewählten, sondern unter gegebenen und überlieferten Umständen. Die Tradition aller toten Geschlechter lastet wie ein Alp auf dem Gehirn der Lebenden." — *Op. cit.*, 2d ed., p. 26.

[2] These articles have recently been collected and published in book form. The articles of 1851–52 have appeared under the title, *Revolution and Counter Revolution, or Germany in 1848*. By Karl Marx. Edited by Eleanor Marx Aveling, London, 1896. The letters of 1853–56 are entitled: *The Eastern Question, a Reprint of Letters written 1853–1856, dealing with the Events of the Crimean War*. By Karl Marx. Edited by Eleanor Marx Aveling and Edward Aveling, London, 1897.

politics of continental Europe in the light of his economic theory, and contributed in no mean degree to the enlightenment of the American public. It was not, however, until the appearance in 1859 of his first professedly scientific work, *Contributions to the Criticism of Political Economy*, that Marx endeavored to sum up his doctrine of economic interpretation and to show how this induced him to attempt his analysis of modern industrial society. He tells us that his

"investigation led to the conclusion that legal relations, like the form of government, can be understood neither of and in themselves nor as the result of the so-called general progress of the human mind, but that they are rooted in the material conditions of life. . . . In the social production of their every-day existence men enter into definite relations that are at once necessary and independent of their own volition — relations of production that correspond to a definite stage of their material powers of production. The totality of these relations of production constitutes the economic structure of society — the real basis on which is erected the legal and political edifice and to which there correspond definite forms of social consciousness. The method of production in material existence conditions social, political and mental evolution in general."[1]

And, after speaking of the periods when the old forces are in temporary conflict with the new, Marx proceeds: —

"With the alteration in the economic basis the whole immense superstructure is more or less slowly transformed. In considering such transformations we must always distinguish between the material transformation in the economic conditions of production, of which natural science teaches us, and the legal political, æsthetic or philosophical — in short ideo-

[1] "Meine Untersuchung mündete in dem Ergebniss, dass Rechtsverhältnisse wie Staatsformen, weder aus sich selbst zu begreifen sind, noch aus der sogenannten allgemeinen Entwicklung des menschlichen Geistes, sondern vielmehr in den materiellen Lebensverhältnissen wurzeln. . . . In der gesellschaftlichen Produktion ihres Lebens gehen die Menschen bestimmte, nothwendige, von ihrem Willen unabhängige Verhältnisse ein, Produktionsverhältnisse, die einer bestimmten Entwicklungsstufe ihrer materiellen Produktionskräfte entsprechen. Die Gesammtheit dieser Produktionsverhältnisse bildet die ökonomische Struktur der Gesellschaft, die reale Basis, worauf sich ein juristischer und politischer Ueberbau erhebt, und welcher bestimmte gesellschaftliche Bewusstseinsformen entsprechen. Die Produktionsweise des materiellen Lebens bedingt den socialen, politischen und geistigen Lebensprocess überhaupt." — *Zur Kritik der Politischen Oekonomie*, Erstes Heft (1859), pp. iv, v.

logical forms, in which men become conscious of this conflict and fight it out."[1]

In his great work on *Capital*, published eight years later, although he continually takes it for granted, Marx nowhere formulates this law. While the final chapter contains some interesting economic history of England since the sixteenth century, Marx confines the discussion to a study of the economic results rather than of the wider social or political consequences. Partly for this reason, and partly because the general public did not distinguish between his historical views and his socialistic analysis of existing industrial society, Marx's view of history had at first but slight influence outside of socialistic circles. After his earlier works came to be studied more carefully, the younger Marxists pointed out the real import of the historical principle. But it was not until the publication in 1894, eleven years after the death of Marx, of the third volume of *Capital*, with its wealth

[1] "In der Betrachtung solcher Umwälzungen muss man stets unterscheiden zwischen der materiellen naturwissenschaftlich treu zu konstatirenden Umwälzung in den ökonomischen Produktionsbedingungen und den juristischen, politischen, religiösen, künstlerischen oder philosophischen, kurz ideologischen Formen, worin sich die Menschen dieses Konflikts bewusst werden und ihn ausfechten."—*Zur Kritik der Politischen Oekonomie*, Erstes Heft (1859), p. v.

of historical interpretation, that the continental writers in general realized the significance of the theory; and it is only since that time that the heated controversy has spread throughout the scientific world.[1] Since neither the earlier works of 1847 or 1859 nor any of the later volumes of *Capital* have as yet been translated, the English-speaking public has had only slight opportunity of grasping the real significance of Marx's theory or its corollaries.

In the first volume of *Capital* the only passage in which Marx definitely refers to his fundamental theory is tucked away in a note.[2] Here he compares his theory to that of Darwin, and insists that it is based on the only really materialistic method: —

"A critical history of technology would show how little any of the inventions of the eighteenth century are the work of a single individual. Hitherto there has been no such book. Darwin has interested us in the history of Nature's technology, *i.e.*, in the formation of the organs of plants and animals, which organs serve as instruments of production for sustain-

[1] In the socialistic circles the controversy may be said to date from 1890, when the matter was taken up in the discussions of the programme of the Social Democratic party in Germany.

[2] *Capital* (English translation), II, p. 367, note 1.

ing life. Does not the history of the productive organs of man, of organs that are the material basis of all social organization, deserve equal attention? And would not such a history be easier to compile, since, as Vico says, human history differs from natural history in this, that we have made the former, but not the latter? Technology discloses man's mode of dealing with Nature,—the process of production by which he sustains his life, and thereby also lays bare the mode of formation of his social relations, and of the mental conceptions that flow from them. Every history of religion, even, that fails to take account of this material basis, is uncritical. It is, in reality, much easier to discover by analysis the earthly core of the misty creations of religion, than it is, conversely, to develop from the actual relations of life the corresponding celestialized forms of those relations. The latter is the only materialistic, and therefore the only scientific method. The weak points in the abstract materialism of natural science, a materialism that excludes history and its process, are at once evident from the abstract and ideological conceptions of its spokesmen, whenever they venture beyond the bounds of their own specialty."

It is in the third volume of *Capital* that Marx gives a definite statement of his theory, with some necessary qualifications, inattention to which is partly responsible for some of the objections to the theory. With this extract we may fitly close the series of quotations:[1]

"It is always the immediate relation of the owner of the conditions of production to the immediate producers — a relation each of whose forms always naturally corresponds to a given stage in the methods and conditions of labor, and thus in its social productivity — in which we find the innermost secret, the hidden basis of the entire social structure, and thus also of the political forms. . . . This does not prevent

[1] "Es ist jedesmal das unmittelbare Verhältniss der Eigenthümer der Produktionsbedingungen zu den unmittelbaren Producenten — ein Verhältniss, dessen jedesmalige Form stets naturgemäss einer bestimmten Entwicklungsstufe der Art und Weise der Arbeit, und daher ihrer gesellschaftlichen Produktivkraft entspricht — worin wir das innerste Geheimniss, die verborgene Grundlage der ganzen gesellschaftlichen Construction, und daher auch die politische Form der Souveränetäts- und Abhängigkeitsverhältnisse, kurz, der jedesmaligen specifischen Staatsform finden. Dies hindert nicht, dass dieselbe ökonomische Basis — dieselbe den Hauptbedingungen nach — durch zahllos verschiedene empirische Umstände, Naturbedingungen, Racenverhältnisse, von aussen wirkende geschichtlichen Einflüsse u. s. w. unendliche Variationen und Abstufungen in der Erscheinung zeigen kann, die nur durch Analyse dieser empirisch gegebenen Umstände zu begreifen sind." — *Das Kapital*, III, 2, pp. 324, 325.

this same economic basis in all its essentials from showing in actual life endless variations and gradations due to various empirical facts, natural conditions, racial relations, and external historical influences without number—all of which can be comprehended only by an analysis of these conditions as they are disclosed by experience."

CHAPTER IV

THE ORIGINALITY OF THE THEORY

We have now studied the genesis and development of the doctrine, chiefly in the words of Marx himself. But, it will be asked, how far is the theory of economic interpretation original with Marx?

There are, indeed, abundant traces of the connection between economic causes and legal, political or social conditions to be found in the literature of earlier centuries. Harrington, for instance, in his *Oceana*, tells us that the form of government depends upon the tenure and distribution of land. The very foundation of his whole theory is: "Such as is the proportion or ballance of dominion or property in Land, such is the nature of the Empire."[1] In the eighteenth

[1] "If one man," he proceeds, "be sole Landlord, or overballance the people, he is Grand Signior . . . and his Empire is Absolute Monarchy. If the Few or a Nobility overballance the people, it makes the Gothic ballance and the Empire is mixed Monarchy (as in Spain and Poland). If the whole people be Landlords, or hold the lands so divided among them that no one

century we find writers, like Germain Garnier[1] in France, Dalrymple[2] in England and Möser[3] in Germany, who emphasized the influence of property in land on politics. Especially in the socialists of the second quarter of the nineteenth century we find not infrequent allusions to a similar point of view. Fourier, St. Simon, Proudhon and Blanc naturally call attention to the influence of economic conditions on the immediate politics of the day,[4] and the first foreign historian of French socialism, Lorenz von Stein, elaborated some of their ideas by positing the general principle of the subordina-

man or number of men . . . overballance them, the Empire (without the interposition of force) is a Commonwealth." — *The Commonwealth of Oceana* (1656), p. 4.

[1] In his *De la Propriété dans ses Rapports avec le Droit Politique* (1792).

[2] In his *An Essay toward a General History of Feudal Property in Great Britain* (1757).

[3] In his *Vorrede zur Osnabrückschen Geschichte* (1768). See the interesting article, "Justus Möser als Geschichtsphilosoph," von P. Kampffmeyer, in *Die Neue Zeit*, XVII, 1, pp. 516–524.

[4] As to St. Simon, see P. Barth in *Die Zukunft*, IV, 449, and the same writer's *Die Philosophie der Geschichte als Soziologie* (1897). *Cf. The French Revolution and Modern French Socialism*, by Jessica Peixotto (1901), pp. 219–221. Both Barth and Peixotto exaggerate the influence of St. Simon. For Fourier and Le Chevalier, see Wenckstern's book on *Marx* (1896), pp. 250, 251. For Proudhon, see Mühlberger, *Zur Kentniss des Marxismus* (1894).

tion of the political to the economic life.[1] The early minor German socialists, such as Marr, Hess and Grün,[2] as well as here and there other writers,[3] express themselves sporadically in like manner. But if originality can properly be claimed only for those thinkers who not alone formulate a doctrine but first recognize its importance and its implications, so that it thereby becomes a constituent element in their whole scientific system, there is no question that Marx must be recognized as in the truest sense the

[1] Stein's views were first advanced in 1842, in *Der Socialismus und Communismus des heutigen Frankreichs.* In a later work, published in 1850, *Geschichte der socialen Bewegung in Frankreich,* he developed more fully his idea of society as the community in its economic organization, and of social, *i.e.*, economic growth as the basis of legal and political life. This produced a decided effect on Gneist, and through him on much of modern German historical jurisprudence. But Stein's doctrine exerted little influence on economic thought or historical investigation in general.

[2] For some of their statements, see G. Adler, *Die Grundlagen der Karl Marx'schen Kritik der Bestehenden Volkswirthschaft* (1887), pp. 214–226. For the more general views of these German socialists, see G. Adler, *Die Geschichte der ersten Socialpolitischen Arbeiterbewegung in Deutschland* (1885).

[3] *Cf.* a remarkable paragraph in the work of the deservedly forgotten Lavergne-Peguilhen, *Die Bewegungs- und Produktionsgesetze* (1838), p. 225, to which Brentano first called attention. Mehring has pointed out the slight importance to be attached to this advocate of the feudal-romantic school, in his *Die Lessing Legende nebst einem Anhange über den Historischen Materialismus* (1893), pp, 435–441.

originator of the economic interpretation of history.[1]

It may be asked, finally, how far the other founders of scientific socialism, Rodbertus and Lassalle, should share with Marx the honor of originating the doctrine of economic interpretation of history. The question of the priority of view as between Marx and Rodbertus was at one time hotly discussed.[2] The controversy, however, turned chiefly on the specifically socialistic doctrines of labor and surplus value, which have in their essentials nothing to do with the economic interpretation of history. Even as to that point, however, the friends of Rodbertus now concede that the charges originally preferred against Marx were false.[3] So

[1] *Cf.* Woltmann, *Der Historische Materialismus* (1900), p. 24.

[2] The charge that Marx copied from Rodbertus was first made by R. Meyer, *Emancipationskampf des Vierten Standes* (1875), I, 43; 2d ed., 1882, pp. 57 and 83, and was repeated by Rodbertus himself in a letter to J. Zeller in the Tübinger *Zeitschrift für die Gesammte Staatswissenschaft* (1879), p. 219. *Cf.* also *Briefe und Socialpolitische Aufsätze von Dr. Rodbertus-Jagetzow*, herausgegeben von Dr. R. Meyer, n.d. [1880], p. 134. The charge was triumphantly refuted by Engels in the preface to *Das Elend der Philosophie*, Deutsch von E. Bernstein (1885), and more fully in the preface to the second (German) volume of *Das Kapital* (1885), pp. viii–xxi.

[3] *Cf.* A. Wagner, in the Introduction to the third volume of *Aus dem Literarischen Nachlass von Dr. Karl Rodbertus-Jagetzow*,

far as the economic interpretation of history is concerned, there is no claim that Rodbertus originated or even maintained the doctrine.[1]

With reference to Lassalle, it would hardly be necessary to refer to the matter at all, were it not for the fact that a prominent English economist has recently implied that the doctrine is first found in his writings.[2] As a matter of fact, it is now conceded by the ablest students of socialism that Lassalle originated none of the important points in theory, even though it is true that without the marvellous practical sagacity of Lassalle the world at large would probably have heard but little of Marx and Rodbertus. The International, in the hands of Marx, was a fiasco; practical socialism, in the hands of Lassalle, became a powerful

herausgegeben von Adolph Wagner und Theophil Kozak (1885), p. xxxi.

[1] *Cf.* A. Wagner, in his *Grundlegung der Politischen Oekonomie*, II (3d ed., 1894), pp. 281, 282, where Marx is described as proceeding "einseitig entwicklungsgesetzlich, mit den Hilfsmitteln seiner materialistischen Geschichtsauffassung," while Rodbertus argues "ohne die geschichtlichen und dialectischen Hilfsmittel von Marx." *Cf.* also the essay of Kautsky "Das 'Kapital' von Rodbertus," in *Die Neue Zeit*, II (1884), p. 350.

[2] Bonar, *Philosophy and Political Economy* (1893), pp. 350, 351, quoting from Lassalle's *Workmen's Programme of 1862*. All the points mentioned by Mr. Bonar are found in Marx's books of 1847 and 1859.

political and social force. But while Lassalle was a great agitator and statesman, he was not a constructive thinker — in economics, at all events; and while Marx was a failure in practical life, he was a giant as a closet philosopher.[1]

[1] It is much to be regretted that Professor Foxwell, in his introduction to the translation of Menger's *The Right to the Whole Produce of Labour* (1899), seems to lend credence to Menger's contention that Marx borrowed his theory of surplus value from the English socialists, without giving them credit. As every one who is familiar with the subject knows, both parts of this statement are erroneous. It was Marx himself who first called attention in detail to the English socialists, quoting extensively from Hopkins [by whom he means Hodgskin], Thompson, Edwards and Bray in *La Misère de la Philosophie* (pp. 49–62); and to compare their theories to that of Marx is like comparing the political economy of Petty to that of Ricardo. It must be remembered, however, that the author of the book in question is not the economist Carl Menger, but his brother Anton, the jurist.

Professor Ashley must have had these passages in mind when he was misled into the hasty characterization of Marx as "a man of great ability, but neither so learned nor so original as he appeared." See his *Surveys, Historic and Economic* (1900), p. 25. Those who really know their Marx have no such opinion. Böhm-Bawerk, one of the chief opponents of Marx's theory of surplus value, has often expressed high admiration for his powers, and goes so far as to call him a "philosophical genius" and "an intellectual force of the highest order." See *Karl Marx and the Close of his System*, by Böhm-Bawerk (1898), pp. 148, 221. If for no other reason than for his admirable and profound treatment of the money problem in the second (German) volume of *Das Kapital*, Marx would occupy a prominent place in the history of economics. His earlier works show that he was equally strong in other fields of human thought. As for his learning, it may suffice to call attention to the fact that Marx was the first

Whether or no we agree with Marx's analysis of industrial society, and without attempting as yet to pass judgment upon the validity of his philosophical doctrine, it is safe to say that no one can study Marx as he deserves to be studied — and, let us add, as he has hitherto *not* been studied in England or America — without recognizing the fact that, perhaps with the exception of Ricardo, there has been no more original, no more powerful, and no more acute intellect in the entire history of economic science.

writer to study in detail the history of early English economic thought, as well as the first economist to make an effective investigation based on the English blue books.

CHAPTER V

THE ELABORATION OF THE THEORY

In the preceding chapters we have studied the genesis and the early formulation of the doctrine of historical materialism. Before proceeding to discuss its applications it may be well to obviate some misunderstanding, by directing attention to what might be called not so much the modifications, as the further elaboration, of the theory.

In saying that the modes of production condition all social life, Marx sometimes leads us to believe that he refers only to the purely technical or technological modes of production. There are, however, abundant indications in his writings to show that he really had in mind the conditions of production in general.[1] This becomes especially important in discussing the earlier stages of civilization, where great changes

[1] The criticisms of Masaryk, *Die Philosophischen und Sociologischen Grundlagen des Marxismus* (1899), pp. 99–100, and of Weisengrün, *Der Marxismus und das Wesen der Sozialen Frage* (1900), p. 86, on this point are without foundation.

occurred in the general relations of production, without much specific alteration in the technical processes. The younger Marxists have devoted much time and ability to the elucidation of this point.

In the first place, even though it is claimed that changes in technique are the causes of social progress, we must be careful not to take too narrow a view of the term. The adherents of the theory point out that when we speak of technique in social life we must include not only the technical processes of extracting the raw material and of fashioning it into a finished product, but also the technique of trade and transportation, the technical methods of business in general, and the technical processes by which the finished product is distributed to the final consumer. Marx intimated this repeatedly, and Engels has stated it clearly in a letter, in which he sums up the ideas for which he and Marx contended:—

"We understand by the economic relations, which we regard as the determining basis of the history of society, the methods by which the members of a given society produce their means of support and exchange the products among each other, so far as the division of labor exists. The whole technique of production and of transportation is thus included. Furthermore, this technique, according to our view, determines the methods of exchange, the distribution of products and, hence, after the dissolution of gentile society, the division of society into classes, the relations of personal control and subjection, and thus the existence of the state, of politics, of law, *etc.* . . . Although technique is mainly dependent on the condition of science, it is still more true that science depends on the condition and needs of technique. A technical want felt by society is more of an impetus to science than ten universities."[1]

[1] "Unter den ökonomischen Verhältnissen, die wir als bestimmende Basis der Geschichte der Gesellschaft ansehen, verstehen wir die Art und Weise, worin die Menschen einer bestimmten Gesellschaft ihren Lebensunterhalt produzieren und die Produkte untereinander austauschen (soweit Teilung der Arbeit besteht). Also die gesamte Technik der Produktion und des Transports ist da einbegriffen. Diese Technik bestimmt nach unserer Auffassung auch die Art und Weise des Austausches, weiterhin die Verteilung der Produkte und damit, nach der Auflösung der Gentilgesellschaft, auch die Einteilung der Klassen, damit die Herrschafts- und Knechtschaftsverhältnisse, damit Staat, Politik, Recht, *etc.* Wenn die Technik, wie sie sagen, ja grösstenteils vom Stande der Wissenschaft abhängig ist, so noch weit mehr dieses vom Stande und den Bedürfnissen der Technik. Hat die Gesellschaft ein technisches Bedürfniss, so hilft das die Wissenschaft mehr voran als zehn Univeisitäten." — Letter of 1894 in *Der Sozialistische Akademiker* (1895), p. 373. Reprinted in L. Woltmann, *Der Historische Materialismus* (1900), p. 248.

The term "technical" must thus be broadened to include the whole series of relations between production and consumption. It is for this reason that we speak not so much of the technical interpretation of history — which would lead to misunderstanding — as of the economic interpretation of history.

The originators of the theory, moreover, go still further. When they speak of the materialistic or economic conception of history, they not only refuse to identify "economic" with "technical" in the narrow sense, but they do not even mean to imply that "economic" excludes physical factors. It is obvious, for instance, that geographical conditions, to some degree and under certain circumstances, affect the facts of production. To the extent that Buckle pointed this out, he was in thorough accord with Marx; but the geographical conditions, as Marx has himself maintained, form only the limits within which the methods of production can act. While a change of geographical conditions may prevent the adoption of new methods of production, precisely the same geographical conditions are often compatible with entirely different methods of production. Thus, Marx tells us: —

"It is not the mere fertility of the soil, but the differentiation of the soil, the variety of its natural products, the changes of the seasons, which form the physical basis for the social division of labor, and which, by changes in the natural surroundings, spur man on to the multiplication of his wants, his capabilities, his means and modes of labor. It is the necessity of bringing a natural force under the control of society, of economizing, of appropriating or subduing it on a large scale by the work of man's hand, that first plays the decisive part in the history of industry."[1]

He goes on to explain, however, that "favorable natural conditions alone give us only the possibility, never the reality," of definite economic methods of production and distribution of wealth. In the same way, Engels concedes that the geographical basis must be included in enumerating the economic conditions, but contends that its importance must not be exaggerated.

This is, however, by no means the most important elaboration of the theory. In the interval that elapsed between the first statement of the theory in the forties and the death

[1] *Capital* (English translation), p. 523.

of Marx, the founders of the doctrine had little reason to moderate their statements. After the death of Marx, however, and especially when the theory began to be actively discussed in the social-democratic congresses, the extreme claims of the orthodox Marxists began to arouse dissent even in the ranks of the socialists themselves. Partly as a result of this, partly because of outside criticism, Engels now wrote a series of letters in which he endeavored to phrase his statement of the theory so as to meet some of the criticisms. In these letters[1] he maintained that Marx had often been misunderstood, and that neither he himself nor Marx ever meant to claim an absolute validity for economic considerations to the exclusion of all other factors. He pointed out that economic actions are not only physical actions, but human actions, and that a man acts as an economic agent through the use of his head as well as of his hands.

[1] Engels's letters, written to various correspondents between 1890 and 1894, appeared originally in two newspapers, the *Leipziger Volkszeitung* (1895), no. 250, and *Der Sozialistische Akademiker*, October 1 and 15, 1895. They have been reprinted, although not all of them in any one place, by Woltmann, *Der Historische Materialismus* (1900), pp. 242–250; by Masaryk, *Die Grundlagen des Marxismus* (1899), pp. 104; by Mehring, *Geschichte der Deutschen Sozialdemokratie*, zweiter Theil (2d ed.), p. 556; and by Greulich, *Ueber die Materialistische Geschichtsauffassung* (1897), p. 7.

The mental development of man, however, is affected by many conditions; at any given time the economic action of the individual is influenced by his whole social environment, in which many factors have played a rôle. Engels confessed that Marx and he were "partly responsible for the fact that the younger men have sometimes laid more stress on the economic side than it deserves," and he was careful to point out that the actual form of the social organization is often determined by political, legal, philosophical and religious theories and conceptions. In short, when we read the latest exposition of their views by one of the founders themselves, it almost seems as if the whole theory of economic interpretation had been thrown overboard.

It would be a mistake, however, to suppose that these concessions, undeniably significant as they are, involved in the minds of the leaders an abandonment of the theory. Engels continued to emphasize the fundamental significance of the economic life in the wider social life. The upholders of the doctrine remind us that, whatever be the action and reaction of social forces at any given time, it is the conditions of production, in the widest sense of the term, that are chiefly responsible for the basic permanent changes in the condition of society. Thus, Engels tells us that we must broaden our conception of the economic factor so as to include among the economic conditions, not only the geographical basis, but the actually transmitted remains of former economic changes, which have often survived only through tradition, or *vis inertiæ*, as well as the whole external environment of this particular form. He even goes so far as to declare the race itself to be an economic factor. And while he still stoutly contends that the political, legal, religious, literary and artistic development rests on the economic, he points out that they all react upon one another and on the economic foundation. "It is not that the economic situation is the cause, in the sense of being the only active agent, and that everything else is only a passive result. It is, on the contrary, a case of mutual action on the basis of the economic necessity, which in last instance always works itself out."[1]

[1] "Ferner sind einbegriffen unter den ökonomischen Verhältnissen die geographische Grundlage, worauf diese sich abspielen, und die thatsächlich überlieferten Reste früherer ökonomischer Entwicklungsstufen, die sich forterhalten haben, oft nur durch Tradition oder *vis inertiae*, natürlich auch das diese Gesellschaftsform nach aussenhin umgebende Milieu. . . .

"Wir sehen die ökonomischen Bedingungen als das in letzter

A controversy that has arisen since Engels's death may serve to bring out the thought more clearly. A number of suggestive writers, of whom Gumplowicz [1] is perhaps the most important, have attempted to explain some of the leading facts in human development by the existence of racial characteristics and race contests. Yet we now have an interesting work by a Frenchman, who does not even profess himself an advocate of the economic interpretation of history, maintaining, with some measure of success, that the majority of different racial characteristics are the results of socio-economic changes which are themselves referable to physico-economic causes. Demolins, the chief representative to-day of the school of LePlay, has — at least, so far as appears from his writings — never even heard of Marx or his theory, and we find in his work very little of the detail

Instanz die geschichtliche Entwicklung Bedingende an. Aber die Rasse ist selbst ein ökonomischer Faktor. . . . Die politische, rechtliche, philosophische, religiöse, litterarische, künstlerische, *etc.*, Entwicklung beruht auf der ökonomischen. Aber sie alle reagieren auch auf einander und auf der ökonomischen Basis. Es ist nicht, dass die ökonomische Lage Ursache, allein aktiv ist und alles andere nur passive Wirkung. Sondern es ist Wechselwirkung auf Grundlage der in letzter Instanz stets sich durchsetzenden ökonomischen Notwendigkeit. . . ." — Letter of 1894, *Der Sozialistische Akademiker*.

[1] *Der Rassenkampf*.

of the class conflict which primarily interested the socialists. But while Demolins[1] reverts in essence to what might be called the commercio-geographical explanation of history, he is careful to point out how the conditions of physical life affect the methods and relations of production, and how these in turn are largely responsible for the differentiation of mankind into the racial types that have played a rôle in history. Thus, from his point of view, the race is largely an economic product, and we begin to understand what Engels meant when he declared the race itself to be an economic factor.

The theory of economic interpretation thus expounded by Engels must be considered authoritative. He tells us that Marx never really regarded the situation in any other light. Nevertheless, it cannot be denied that there are passages in Marx which seem to be more extreme, and which represent the doctrine in that cruder form which is so frequently met with among his uncritical followers. We are bound, however, to give him the benefit of the doubt, and we must not forget that when a new theory supposed to involve far-reaching prac-

[1] Edmond Demolins, *Comment la Route crée le Type Social, Essai de Géographie Sociale*, n.d. [1901].

tical consequences is first propounded, the apparent needs of the situation often result in an overstatement, rather than an understatement, of the doctrine.

We understand, then, by the theory of economic interpretation of history, not that all history is to be explained in economic terms alone, but that the chief considerations in human progress are the social considerations, and that the important factor in social change is the economic factor. Economic interpretation of history means, not that the economic relations exert an exclusive influence, but that they exert a preponderant influence in shaping the progress of society.

So much for a preliminary statement of the real content of the economic conception of history, as explained and elaborated by the founders themselves. In a subsequent chapter we shall revert to this point and attempt to analyze somewhat more closely the actual connection between the economic and the wider social relations of mankind.

CHAPTER VI

RECENT APPLICATIONS OF THE THEORY

LET us now proceed to study some of the applications that have been made of the theory of the economic interpretation of history. We can pursue this study without prejudicing the final decision as to the truth of the doctrine in its entirety; for it is obvious that we may refuse to admit the validity of the theory as a philosophical explanation of progress as a whole, and yet be perfectly prepared to admit that in particular cases the economic factor has played an important rôle. It is natural, however, that the economic influence in any given set of facts should be emphasized primarily by those whose general philosophical attitude would predispose them to search for economic causes. It will not surprise us, then, to find that much good work in this direction has been accomplished by the originators of the theory and their followers.

Marx himself made no mean contribution to

the facts. Some of his statements are erroneous, and not a few of his historical explanations are farfetched and exaggerated; but there remains a considerable substratum of truth in his contributions to the subject. Of these contributions the most familiar is the account of the transition from feudal to modern society, due to the genesis in the seventeenth century of capital as a dominant industrial factor and to the industrial revolution of the eighteenth century. It was Marx who first clearly pointed out the nature of the domestic system and its transformation into the factory system of our age, with the attendant change from the local to the national market, and from this in turn to the world market. It was Marx, again, who called attention to the essential difference between the economic life of classic antiquity and that of modern times, showing that, while capital played by no means an insignificant rôle in ancient times, it was commercial and not industrial capital, and that much of Greek and Roman history is to be explained in the light of this fact. It was Marx, too, who first disclosed the economic forces which were chiefly responsible for the political changes of the middle of the nineteenth century. And, finally, while Marx had originally devoted comparatively little attention to primitive civilization, we now know that in his manuscript notes he applied his doctrine in a suggestive way to the very first stages of social evolution.[1]

It is perhaps in the early history of mankind that the most signal additions to our knowledge have been made by recent writers. The pioneer in this field was our great compatriot Morgan. Morgan was really the first to explain the early forms of human association and to trace society through the stages of the horde, the clan, the family and the state. Moreover, although he did not work it out in detail or give his theory any name, there is no doubt that he independently advanced the doctrine of the economic interpretation of history, without being aware of the fact that it applied to anything but the early stages. Because of the great neglect by subsequent writers of this part of Morgan's achievements, it is necessary to call attention to it at somewhat greater length.

Morgan starts out with the guarded statement that it is "probable that the great epochs

[1] These notes are used by Engels in his *Der Ursprung der Familie, des Privateigenthums und des Staats* (1884). See Preface to first edition.

of human progress have been identified more or less directly with the enlargement of the sources of subsistence."[1] The great epochs of which he speaks, however, cease, in his opinion, with the introduction of field agriculture.[2] He discusses the assumption of original promiscuity in the human race, and maintains that, while it probably existed at first, it is not likely that it was long continued in the horde, because the latter would break up into smaller groups for subsistence and fall into consanguine families.[3] In his treatment of the dependence of early man upon the physical characteristics of the food supply, he takes up in turn the early natural subsistence upon fruits and roots, the connection of fish subsistence with savagery and migration, the relations between the discovery of cereals, the cessation of cannibalism and the reliance on a meat and milk diet, the connection between the domestication of animals and pastoral society, and, finally, the transition of what he calls horticulture into agriculture.[4] In all this we seem to be get-

[1] Lewis H. Morgan, *Ancient Society* (1877). The following quotations are from the edition of 1878, p. 19. *Cf.* p. 9.

[2] *Ibid.*, p. 26.

[3] *Ibid.*, p. 418.

[4] *Ibid.*, pp. 20–26. Morgan's "horticulture" is really the same as the "hoeculture" or "hackculture" which has recently

ting little beyond Buckle. What differentiates Morgan entirely from Buckle, however, is the fact that, while the latter confines himself to the simple problem of production, Morgan works out the influence of all these factors upon the social and political constitution and traces the transformation of society to changes in the form and conditions of property.

Although Morgan did not succeed in making thoroughly clear the economic causes of the early tracing of descent from the female line, he did call attention to the connection between the growth of private property and the evolution of the horde into the clan or, as he calls it, the gens.[1] He elucidated still more clearly the causes of the change of descent from the female to the male line, showing how it went hand in hand with the extension of the institution of private property.[2] The account of

been heralded by German writers, like Hahn and Schmoller, as a great discovery of their compatriots. Both terms are ill chosen.

[1] "With the institution of the gens came in the first great rule of inheritance which distributed the effects of a deceased person among his gentiles." — *Ancient Society*, p. 528.

[2] "After domestic animals began to be reared in flocks and herds, becoming thereby a source of subsistence as well as objects of individual property, and after tillage had led to the ownership of houses and lands in severalty, an antagonism would be certain to arise against the prevailing form of gentile inheri-

the development of slavery[1] is perhaps not so novel; but the suggestion of an economic basis for the transition from the clan to the patriarchal family[2] and from the polygamic to the monogamic family[3] was as striking as it was original.

While Morgan was in no way an economist,

tance, because it excluded the owner's children whose paternity was becoming more assured, and gave his property to his gentile kindred. A contest for a new rule of inheritance, shared in by the fathers and their children, would furnish a motive sufficiently powerful to effect the change. With property accumulating in masses, and assuming permanent forms, and with an increased proportion of it held by individual ownership, descent in the female line was certain of overthrow, and the substitution of the male line equally assured. Such a change would leave the inheritance in the gens as before, but it would place children in the gens of their father and at the head of the agnatic kindred." — Lewis H. Morgan, *Ancient Society* (1877), pp. 345–346. *Cf.* p. 531.

[1] *Ibid.*, p. 341, *et passim*.

[2] The patriarchal family is summed up as "an organization of servants and slaves under a patriarch for the care of flocks and herds, for the cultivation of lands and for mutual protection and subsistence. Polygamy was incidental." — *Ibid.*, p. 504. *Cf.* pp. 465–466.

[3] "The growth of property and the desire for its transmission to children was in reality the moving power which brought in monogamy to insure legitimate heirs and to limit their number to the actual progeny of the married pair." — *Ibid.*, p. 477.

"As finally constituted, the monogamian family assured the paternity of children, substituted the individual ownership of real as well as of personal property for joint ownership, and an exclusive inheritance by children instead of agnatic inheritance." — *Ibid.*, p. 505. *Cf.* p. 389.

and had probably never heard either of Marx or of the historical school of economics, his final conclusion as to the relations of private property to social welfare is in substantial agreement with modern views. He tells us that

"since the advent of civilization the outgrowth of property has been so immense, its forms so diversified, its uses so expanding and its management so intelligent in the interests of its owners, that it has become, on the part of the people, an unmanageable power. The human mind stands bewildered in the presence of its own creation. The time will come, nevertheless, when human intelligence will rise to the mastery over property, and define the relations of the state to the property it protects as well as the obligation and the limits of the rights of its owners. The interests of society are paramount to individual interests and the two must be brought into just and harmonious relations."[1]

The greater part of Morgan's book as well as of his other works[2] was, however, devoted

[1] *Ancient Society*, p. 552.

[2] *The League of the Iroquois* (1849, reprinted in 1902); *Systems of Consanguinity and Affinity of the Human Family* (1871); and *Houses and House Life of the American Aborigines* (1881).

to an account of the historical facts themselves, rather than of their economic causes. The controversy which at once sprang up in England, and which has lasted almost to the present time, turned well-nigh exclusively upon the first set of considerations. When scientists were not agreed upon the facts it would seem useless to speculate about the causes of the facts. The trend given to the discussion by this early controversy is largely responsible for the fact that until very recently writers on sociology or social history have almost completely neglected the economic aspect of the transitions which they describe.[1] But, although some parts of Morgan's theory — like the details of the earliest consanguine family and the perhaps somewhat hasty generalization as to primitive promiscuity — have been modified,

[1] This is true of McLennan, Westermaarck, Starcke, Tyler, Lumholtz, Post and many others. It is true also, although to a somewhat less degree, of my honored colleague, Professor Giddings. Almost the only passage of importance for our purposes in his *Principles of Sociology* (1896) is the one on p. 266: "It seems to be an economic condition which in the lowest communities determines the duration of marriage and probably also the line of descent through mothers or fathers." *Cf.*, however, in addition, pp. 276, 288 and 296. In a more recent article Professor Giddings substantially concedes that "these writers [Marx and his followers] may be held to have made good their main contention." — *International Monthly*, II (1900), p. 548.

the substance of his account of the uterine or maternal clan and of its development into the tribe and the state, as well as of the dependence of the transition upon changes in the forms of property, have become incorporated into the accepted material of modern science.

It was not, however, until the German advocates of the economic interpretation of history took the matter up that Morgan's real importance was recognized. Engels published in 1884 his *Origin of the Family*, in which he showed that Morgan's views marked a distinct advance upon those of Bachofen and McLennan, and claimed that the English archæologists of the day had really adopted Morgan's theory without giving him credit. Turning from the account of the development to its causes, Engels accepted all of Morgan's conclusions as to the early uterine society and the development of monogamy, but carried them one step further by combining, as he tells us, Morgan and Marx. Engels ascribed the transformation of gentile society to the first great social division of labor — the separation of pastoral tribes from the rest of society. This in itself gave rise to intertribal exchange as a permanent factor in economic life, and it was not long before intertribal exchange led to barter between individuals — a barter chiefly in cattle and natural products. With the transition from common to private property in such movables, the ground was prepared, on the one hand, for slavery and, on the other, for the downfall of the matriarchate. As private property increased we find the second great step in the division of labor, — the separation of manual industry from agriculture. Exchange now becomes an exchange of commodities, and with the economic supremacy of the male there appear the patriarchate and then the monogamic family. Finally, comes the third step in the division of labor, — the rise of the merchant class, with the use of metallic money. The growth of capital, even if it be mercantile capital (as against the original cattle capital), ushers in a state of affairs with which the old gentile organization is no longer able to cope; and thus we find the origin of the political organization, the genesis of the state. In Greece, in Rome and in the Teutonic races of the early middle ages this transition is a matter of record; but no one before Morgan and Engels had been able to explain it intelligibly.

The hints thrown out by Morgan and Engels have been worked up by a number of writers, few of whom can be classed as socialists. At first the professed sociologists paid but little attention to the matter. With Kovalevsky, in 1890, we begin the series of those who attempted to prove a somewhat closer connection between the family and private property.[1] In 1896 Grosse devoted a separate volume to the subject[2] and brought out some new points as to the influence of economic conditions upon the character of the family, especially in the case of nomadic peoples and the early agriculturists. In the same year Professor Hildebrand published an admirable work on *Law and Custom in the Different Economic Stages*, in which, although not neglecting the earlier phases of social life, he laid the emphasis on the economic basis of the primitive agricultural community.[3] For the still earlier period noteworthy work has been done by Cunow. After having prepared the way by a study of the sys-

[1] Maxime Kovalevsky, "Tableau des origines et de l'évolution de la famille et de la propriété," *Skrifter utgifna af Lorenska Stiftelsen* (Stockholm, 1890).

[2] *Die Formen der Familie und die Formen der Wirthschaft* (1896).

[3] *Recht und Sitte auf den Verschiedenen Wirthschaftlichen Kulturstufen*, Erster Theil (1896).

tems of consanguinity among the Australians[1] Cunow published in 1898 a series of articles on the economic basis of the matriarchate.[2] He emphasized the essential weakness, from the historical point of view, of the ordinary classification into hunting, pastoral and agricultural stages.[3] Beginning, however, with the hunting stage, Cunow maintains that the earliest form of organization rests on the supremacy of the man, which is not by any means the same thing as the supremacy of the father; for the polygamic or monogamic family which forms the basis of the patriarchal system was of much later development. In the early stages we may have a uterine society — that is, a tracing of descent through the mother — but we have no matriarchate.[4] Cunow gives the economic rea-

[1] *Die Verwandschaftsorganisationen der Australneger* (1894).

[2] "Die ökonomischen Grundlagen der Mutterherrschaft," in *Die Neue Zeit*, XVI, p. 1. A French version appeared in *Le Devenir Social*, V (1898), pp. 42, 146, 330, under the title "Les bases économiques du matriarcat."

[3] *Die Neue Zeit*, XVI, p. 108. Cunow, however, does not remind us that all this had been pointed out in 1884 by Dargun in his admirable study, which is not so well known as it ought to be: "Ursprung und Entwicklungsgeschichte des Eigenthums," in the *Zeitschrift für Vergleichende Rechtswissenschaft*, V, especially pp. 59–61. Professor Giddings, in his article in the *Political Science Quarterly* for June, 1901 (XVI, 204), alludes to the older theory as based on "the Mother-Goose philosophy of history." Dargun and Cunow are the writers who have emancipated us.

[4] *Die Neue Zeit*, XVI, p. 115.

sons which explain this tracing of the descent through the female, and shows how, under certain conditions, she becomes more sought after until finally she attains such an economic importance that the matriarchate itself develops.[1] Incidentally he traces the connection between the female and early agriculture, and explains how her growing importance, both in and out of the home, exerted a decided influence upon the early division of labor. The matriarchate is shown very clearly to be largely an economic product.[2]

In 1901 Cunow followed up his exposition by another series of essays on "The Division of Labor and the Rights of Women."[3] Here he points out the error of the usual statement that agriculture is a condition precedent to a disappearance of the nomadic life. On the contrary, maintains Cunow, a certain degree of stationary settled activity is a condition precedent to the transition to agriculture.[4] Agriculture, however, may develop either out of the

[1] *Die Neue Zeit*, XVI, pp. 141, 176, 209.

[2] *Ibid.*, pp. 238, 241.

[3] "Arbeitstheilung und Frauenrecht; zugleich ein Beitrag zur materialistischen Geschichtsauffassung," in *Die Neue Zeit*, XIX, p. 1.

[4] *Ibid.*, p. 103.

pastoral stage or out of the hunting stage, and in each case the activity of the female is of cardinal importance. The female is not only the primitive tiller of the soil, but also the creator of the earliest house industry, which plays such a distinctive rôle in primitive barter.[1] The earliest division of labor rests on the principle that the female attends to the vegetable sustenance, the man to the animal diet, and on this fundamental distinction all the other social arrangements are built up. Marriage, for a long time, is not an ethical community of ideal interests, but very largely an economic or labor relation.[2]

Of much the same character as this investigation are the attempts made still more recently to supply an economic explanation for the origin of totemism[3] and to study the economic causes of slavery. Especially on the

[1] "Arbeitstheilung und Frauenrecht; zugleich ein Beitrag zur materialistischen Geschichtsauffassung," in *Die Neue Zeit*, XIX, pp. 152, 180.

[2] *Ibid.*, p. 276.

[3] Dr. Julius Pikler: *Der Ursprung des Totemismus; ein Beitrag zur Materialistischen Geschichtstheorie* (Berlin, 1900). A somewhat different, but equally "materialistic," interpretation has been given by Frazer, in the *Fortnightly Review* for 1899, and by Professor Giddings, in a note on "The Origin of Totemism and Exogamy" in the *Annals of the American Academy of Political and Social Science*, XIV, p. 274.

latter topic our knowledge of the early conditions has been greatly increased by the detailed study of Nieboer.[1] Nieboer, who accepts the theory of the brilliant Italian economist Loria, has overturned many of the former notions on the subject and has studied slavery, not only, as most writers have done, in the agricultural stage of society, but also in the hunting, fishing and pastoral stages. Coming to the later period of classic antiquity, Ciccotti has shed considerable light on the origin and development of slavery in Greece, as well as in Rome, and has traced the connection between this fundamental fact and the entire political and social history.[2] Other writers, such as Francotte[3] and Pöhlmann,[4] have considered more in detail the economic status of Greece and its influence on national and international conditions.

[1] Dr. H. J. Nieboer: *Slavery as an Industrial System* (The Hague, 1900). See the review of this work in the *Political Science Quarterly*, September, 1901.

[2] Ettore Ciccotti: *Il Tramonto della Schiavitù nel Mondo Antico* (Torino, 1899). The suggestive sketch of the whole topic by Eduard Meyer, in his address *Die Sklaverei im Alterthum* (1898), suffers in some important points from the fact that the well-known historian is only imperfectly acquainted with the results of recent economic studies.

[3] Francotte, *L'Industrie dans la Grèce Ancienne* (1901).

[4] Pöhlmann, *Geschichte des Antiken Sozialismus und Communismus* (1901).

In the case of Roman history the relation between the land question and national progress has always been so obvious that such historians as Nitzsch and Mommsen did not have to wait for the rise of the school of economic interpretation. Even in the case of Rome, however, good work has since then been done, especially in the imperial period, in emphasizing the controlling influence of economic factors on the general devolopment.[1] So, also, some neglected points in the history of Hebrew antiquity have been brought out by writers like Beer and Mehring.[2]

When we come to more recent periods of history there is an embarrassment of riches. The economic forces which were instrumental in shaping the transition from feudal to modern society are so obvious that the historians have for some time been laying stress on economic interpretation almost without knowing it. This is true, for instance, in the treatment

[1] *Cf.* the series of essays by Paul Ernst on "Die sozialen Zustände im römischen Reiche vor dem Einfall der Barbaren," in *Die Neue Zeit*, XI (1893), p. 2, and the suggestive book of Deloume, *Les Manieurs d'Argent à Rome* (1892).

[2] M. Beer, "Ein Beitrag zur Geschichte des Klassenkampfes im hebräischen Alterthum," *Die Neue Zeit*, XI (1893), 1, p. 444. For similar studies by Kautsky and Lafargue, see Mehring, *Die Lessing-Legende*, p. 481.

of the military system, which has been clearly described by Bürkli in his account of the transition in Switzerland.[1] One of the most accomplished of Belgian historians, Des Marez, has recently voiced his conviction that "no one can investigate the deeper causes that have influenced the peoples between the Rhine and the North Sea without perceiving that it is above all the economic conditions, and not racial, linguistic or other factors, that have determined national progress."[2]

The newer view has led investigators to accentuate the economic factor not only in the Crusades[3] but also in the Reformation with the victory of Calvinism and Puritanism.[4] The

[1] Karl Bürkli, *Der Wahre Winkelried; die Taktik der Alten Urschweizer*, 1886. See especially pp. 143–184. *Cf.* also the same author's *Der Ursprung der Eidgenossenschaft aus der Markgenossenschaft und die Schlacht am Morgarten*, 1891. In this monograph emphasis is laid on the economic origin of the Swiss democracy in general.

[2] G. Des Marez, *Les Luttes Sociales en Flandre au Moyen Âge*, 1900, p. 7.

[3] *Cf.* the article by Prutz, "The Economic Development of Western Europe under the Influence of the Crusades," *The International Monthly*, IV (August, 1901), 2, p. 251.

[4] See especially Engels, *Der deutsche Bauernkrieg;* Bernstein's essay on "The Socialistic Currents during the English Revolution" in *Die Geschichte des Sozialismus in Einzeldarstellungen*, I, 2, and published as a separate work under the title *Communistische und Demokratisch-socialistische Strömungen in der Eng-*

professed historians themselves have been so far influenced by the movement that Lamprecht, one of the most distinguished of German scholars, has recently made the economic factor the very foundation of the entire political and social development of mediæval Germany.[1] In the acrimonious discussion that this "audacious" move has engendered, and which is not yet concluded, the gradual triumph of the newer tendency seems by no means improbable.[2]

When we approach the centuries nearer our own time, it has almost become a commonplace to explain in economic terms the political transition of England in the eighteenth century, as well as the French and American revolutions. To take only a few examples from more recent

lischen Revolution des XVII Jahrhunderts, 1895; Kautsky, *Communism in Central Europe in the Time of the Reformation*, 1897, and Belfort Bax's study on the *Social Side of the German Reformation*, of which two volumes have thus far appeared under the titles: *German Society at the Close of the Middle Ages*, 1894, and *The Peasants' War*, 1899.

[1] Lamprecht, *Deutsche Geschichte*. Few economists or economic historians would deny, however, that Professor Lamprecht has been unfortunate in selecting as the important factor what is generally regarded as a secondary rather than a primary phenomenon. The change from a natural to a money economy, which Lamprecht emphasizes, is itself the result of antecedent economic forces.

[2] Lamprecht's general views may be found in his *Alte und Neue Richtung in der Geschichtswissenschaft* and *Was ist Kul-*

events, it is no longer open to doubt that the democracy of the nineteenth century is largely the result of the industrial revolution; that the entire history of the United States to the Civil War was at the bottom a struggle between two economic principles; that the Cuban insurrection against Spain, and thus indirectly the Spanish-American War, was the outcome of the sugar situation; or, finally, that the condition of international politics at present is dominated by economic considerations. Wherever we turn in the maze of recent historical investigation, we are confronted by the overwhelming importance attached by the younger and abler scholars to the economic factor in political and social progress.

turgeschichte? 1896. A list of some recent articles on the controversy may be found in Ashley, *Surveys, Historic and Economic*, p. 29. To these may now be added the article of Below in the *Historische Zeitschrift*, LXXXVI (1900), 1, and the French books of Lacombe, *De l'Histoire considérée comme Science*, 1894 and Seignobos, *La Méthode Historique appliquée aux Sciences Sociales*, 1901. Perhaps the most striking work of this nature that has been accomplished by an American scholar is the article of E. V. D. Robinson, "War and Economics in History and Theory," *Political Science Quarterly*, XV (1900), pp. 581–586.

PART II

CRITICISM OF THE THEORY OF ECONOMIC INTERPRETATION

CHAPTER I

FREEDOM AND NECESSITY

We come now to the most important part of the subject, — a consideration, namely, of the objections that have been urged to the doctrine here under discussion. Some of these objections, as we shall learn later, are indeed weighty but others possess only a partial validity. Yet the emphasis is commonly put by the critics of economic interpretation on the weak, rather than on the sound, arguments. It will be advisable, then, to consider first and at greater length some of these alleged objections, reserving for later treatment those criticisms which possess greater force.

Among the criticisms commonly advanced the more usual may be summarized as follows: first, that the theory of economic interpretation is a fatalistic theory, opposed to the doctrine of free will and overlooking the importance of great men in history; second, that it rests on the assumption of "historical laws" the very existence of which is open to question; third, that it is socialistic; fourth, that it neglects the ethical and spiritual forces in history; fifth, that it leads to absurd exaggerations.

It will be observed that these criticisms fall into two categories. The one category takes exception, not only to the economic interpretation of history, but to the general social interpretation of history. The other class of objections does not deny that the controlling forces of progress are social in character, but contends that we must not confound economic with social considerations and that the economic factor is of no more importance than any of the other social factors. In the above list the first and second criticisms are to be included in the former category; the third and fifth in the latter; while the fourth criticism is so broad that it falls partly in each category.

We begin with the first class of criticisms because some writers think that they are triumphantly refuting the economic interpretation of history, when they are in reality directing their weapons against a far more comprehensive structure of ideas, which very few of the opponents of the economic interpretation of history would like to see demolished. Let us consider, then, the objection that the doctrine is fatalistic, that it is opposed to the theory of free will, and that it overlooks the importance of great men in history.[1]

It is obvious that this is not the place to enter into a general philosophical discussion of determinism. For our purposes it is sufficient to state that if by freedom of the will we simply mean the power to decide as to an action, there is no necessary clash with the doctrine of economic or social interpretation. The denial of this statement involves a fallacy, which in its general aspects has been neatly hit off by Huxley:—

"Half the controversies about the freedom of the will . . . rest upon the absurd presumption that the proposition "I can do as I like" is contradictory to the doctrine of necessity. The answer is: nobody doubts that, at any rate within certain limits, you can do as you like. But what determines your likings and dislik-

[1] Professor Ashley, for instance, resolves the whole question into "another form of the eternal problem of the universe: Necessity or Free Will." *Surveys, Historic and Economic*, p. 26. Mr. Bonar, in his temperate and interesting article on the subject, seems to come dangerously near to this position in speaking of the "helplessness" of society. See "Old Lights and New in Economic Study," *Economic Journal*, viii, p. 444.

ings? . . . The passionate assertion of the consciousness of their freedom, which is the favorite refuge of the opponents of the doctrine of necessity, is mere futility, for nobody denies it. What they really have to do if they would upset the necessarian argument, is to prove that they are free to associate any emotion whatever with any idea however, to like pain as much as pleasure; vice as much as virtue; in short, to prove that, whatever may be the fixity of order of the universe of things, that of thought is given over to chance."[1]

In other words, every man has will power and may decide to act or to refrain from acting, thus showing that he is in this sense a free agent. But whether he decides in the one way or the other, there are certain causes operating within the organism which are responsible for the decision. The function of science is to ascertain what these causes are. All that we know thus far is that every man is what he is because of the influence of environment, past or present. We need not here enter into the biological disputes between the Weissmannist and the Neo-

[1] *Hume, with Helps to the Study of Berkeley*, ch. x. In Huxley's *Collected Essays*, vol. vi, p. 220.

Lamarckian; for, whether we believe with the one that the only factor in progress is the power of natural selection to transmit and strengthen congenital characteristics, or with the other that acquired characteristics are also inherited, we are dealing in each case with the operation of some form of past environment. Neither Weissmannists nor Neo-Lamarckians deny the obvious fact of the influence of present environment on the individual as such.

Since, therefore, man, like everything else, is what he is because of his environment, past and present, — that is, the environment of his ancestors as well as his own, — it is clear that, if we knew all the facts of his past and present environment, we should be in a much better position to foretell with some degree of precision the actions of every human being. Although a man is free to steal or not to steal, we are even now safe in predicting that under ordinary circumstances an honest man will not steal. His congenital and acquired characteristics are such that under certain conditions he will always elect a certain course of action. In the case of physical environment the matter is very simple. While an Eskimo may be perfectly free to go naked, it is not a violent stretch of the fancy to assume that no sane Eskimo will do so as long as he remains in the Arctic regions. When we leave the physical and come to the social environment, as we necessarily do in discussing the doctrine of economic interpretation, the essence of the matter is not much changed.

The theory of social environment, reduced to its simplest elements, means that, even though the individual be morally and intellectually free to choose his own action, the range of his choices will be largely influenced by the circumstances, traditions, manners and customs of the society about him. I may individually believe in polygamy and may be perfectly free to decide whether to take one or two wives; but if I live outside of Utah, the chances are very great that I shall be so far guided in my decision by the law and social custom as to content myself with one spouse. The common saying that a man's religion is formed for him affords another illustration. The son of a Mohammedan may elect to become a Christian, but it is safe to predict that for the immediate future the vast majority of Turks will remain Mohammedans.

The negation of the theory of social environment excludes the very conception of law in the moral disciplines. It would render impossible the existence of statistics, jurisprudence, economics, politics, sociology or even ethics. For what do we mean by a social law? Social law means that amid the myriad decisions of the presumable free agents that compose a given community there can be discovered a certain general tendency or uniformity of action, deviation from which is so slight as not to impair the essential validity of the general statement. In a race of cannibals the abstention by any one savage from human flesh will not influence the history of that tribe; in the present industrial system the offer on the part of any one employer to double the customary wages of his workmen will have no appreciable effect upon the general relations of labor and capital. The controlling considerations are always the social considerations. At bottom, of course, the individual is the unit; and every individual may be conceived as, ideally at least, a free agent. But for individuals living in society the theories that influence progress are the social choices, that is, the choices of the majority. The decision of any one individual is important only to the extent that his influence preponderates with the great majority; and then it is no longer an individual judgment, but becomes that of the majority.[1]

This is the reason why the "great man theory" of history has well-nigh disappeared. No one, indeed, denies the value of great men or the vital importance of what Matthew Arnold calls the remnant. Without the winged thoughts and the decisive actions of the great leaders, the progress of the world would doubtless have been considerably retarded. But few now overlook the essential dependence of the great man upon the wider social environment amid which he has developed.[2]

Aristotle, the greatest thinker of antiquity, defended slavery because slavery was at the time an integral part of the whole fabric of Greek civilization. A Jefferson would be as impossible in Turkey as a Pobyedonostseff

[1] For an application of this doctrine to the theory of economics, see an article by the present writer on "Social Elements in the Theory of Value" in the *Quarterly Journal of Economics* (June, 1901).

[2] In his interesting essay on "Great Men and their Environment" Prof. William James says many things which command assent, especially in connection with the geographical interpretation of history. But he misses the main point, although he hints at it on pp. 226–227. See *The Will to believe and Other Essays* (1897).

in the United States. Pheidias is as unthinkable in China as Lionardo in Canada. On the other hand, the effects ascribed to great men are often largely the result of forces of which they were only the chance vehicles. Cæsar erected the Roman Empire, but the empire would undoubtedly have come ultimately with or without Cæsar. Napoleon for the time transformed the face of Europe, but the France of to-day would in all probability have been in its essentials the same had Napoleon never lived. Washington and Lincoln assuredly exercised the most profound influence on their times, but it is scarcely open to doubt that in the end the Revolution would have succeeded and the Rebellion would have failed, even though Washington and Lincoln had never existed.

While his appearance at a particular moment appears to us a matter of chance, the great man influences society only when society is ready for him. If society is not ready for him, he is called, not a great man, but a visionary or a failure. Just as in animal life the freak or sport works through natural selection as fixed by the environment, so in human life the great man can permanently succeed only if the social environment is ripe. Biologists tell us that variation in the species is the cause of all progress, but that the extreme limit of successful variation from the parent type in any one case does not exceed a small percentage. The great man represents the extreme limit of successful variation in the human race. It is to him that progress seems to be, and in fact often is, in large measure due. But we must not forget that even then the great mass of his characteristics are those of the society about him, and that he is great because he visualizes more truly than any one else the fundamental tendencies of the community in which his lot is cast, and because he expresses more successfully than others the real spirit of the age of which he is the supreme embodiment.[1]

It is, therefore, an obviously incorrect statement of the problem to assert that the theory of economic interpretation, or the theory of social environment of which it is a part, is incom-

[1] An interesting attempt to study in detail the causes of the appearance of great men in a particular country and a particular field has been made by A. Odin, professor at the University of Sofia, in his two-volume work, *Gènèse des Grands Hommes* (1895). The author devotes himself specifically to the great men in French literature and concludes that the social and economic environment, and not the force of heredity or chance, is the capital factor in the phenomenon.

patible with the doctrine of free will. If by determinism we erroneously mean moral fatalism, determinism is not involved at all.[1] To call the general doctrine "economic determinism" as is occasionally done in France, is therefore essentially erroneous. The theory of social environment in no way implies fatalism. Social arrangements are human arrangements, and human beings are, in the sense indicated, free to form decisions and to make social choices; but they will invariably be guided in their decisions by the sum of ideas and impressions which have been transmitted to them through inheritance and environment. So far as great men influence the march of progress, they can do so only to the extent that they can induce the community to accept these new ideas as something in harmony with their surroundings and their aspirations.

Given a certain set of conditions, the great mass of the community will decide to act in a certain way. Social law rests on the obser-

[1] The passage sometimes quoted from Marx, *Das Kapital*, III, 2, p. 355, does not refer to the general problem of determinism, as Masaryk (*Grundlagen des Marxismus*, p. 232) seems to think, but to freedom in the sense of liberation from the necessity of working all day in the factory and having no time for self-improvement.

vation that men will choose a course of action in harmony with what they conceive to be their welfare, and on the further observation that the very idea of an organized community implies that a majority will be found to entertain common ideas of what is their welfare. If the conditions change, the common ideas will change with them. The conditions, so far as they are social in character, are indeed created by men and may be altered by men, so that in last resort there is nothing fatalistic about progress.[1] But it is after all the conditions which, because of their direct action or reaction on individuals, are at any given moment responsible for the general current of social thought.

To the extent, then, that the theory of economic interpretation is simply a part of the general doctrine of social environment, the contention that it necessarily leads to an unreason-

[1] It is impossible to speak in any but respectful terms of Professor James. The limits of our toleration, however, are well-nigh reached when we find such an extreme statement as this: "I cannot but consider the talk of the contemporary sociological school about averages and general causes the most pernicious and immoral of fatalisms." — See the chapter on "The Importance of Individuals," in *The Will to Believe*, p. 262. This apparently shows an egregious misconception of the very nature of social law.

ing fatalism is baseless. Men are the product of history, but history is made by men.[1]

[1] Those interested in the discussion of this point by the socialists may be referred to the articles of Kautsky, Bernstein and Mehring in *Die Neue Zeit*, XVII (1899), 2, pp. 4, 150, 268 and 845. Engels has also touched upon it several times, in his *Anti-Dühring*, in his *Ludwig Feuerbach* (2d ed., 1895), p. 44, and more fully in his letter of 1894 published in *Der Sozialistische Akademiker* (1895), p. 373, and reprinted in Woltmann, *Der Historische Materialismus*, p. 250.

CHAPTER II

HISTORICAL LAW AND SOCIALISM

THE second objection to the theory under discussion is closely related to the first. The economic interpretation of history presupposes that there are historical laws. Yet this is demurred to by some.

Those, however, who deny the existence of historical laws are evidently laboring under a misapprehension. What they obviously mean is that the statement of some particular historical law is false, or that the causes of some definite historical occurrence are so complex and so obscure that it is well-nigh impossible to frame a general explanation. But they cannot mean that historical laws do not exist. The mere fact that we have not discovered a law does not prove that there is none.

For what is meant by a scientific law? A law is an explanatory statement of the actual relations between facts. The processes of human thought enable us to classify the likenesses and differences in the myriad phenomena of life, and to subsume the unity underlying these differences. This unity makes itself known to us under the guise of a causal relation of one phenomenon to another. When we have succeeded in ascertaining the relation of cause and effect we are able to frame the law. But our inability to discover the law does not invalidate the fact of its existence. The relations between the stars existed from the beginning of time; the discovery of the law which enables us to explain these relations is a result of scientific progress.[1]

What is true of the exact sciences is equally true of the social sciences, with the difference that the social sciences are immeasurably more complex because of the greater difficulty in isolating the phenomena to be investigated, and in repeating the experiments. But to deny the existence of social laws, for instance, simply be-

[1] This does not, of course, imply that the law possesses an objective existence apart from our apperceptions. A consideration of this problem belongs to the science of epistemology. The questions of the "Ding an sich" and of the necessary limits of human thought have no place in this discussion; nor have they any bearing upon the particular objection here alluded to. For the contention in question is not that historical laws have no objective existence, but that there is no possibility of our framing an adequate explanation of causal relations.

cause some particular alleged laws may be convicted of unreality would be to repeat the errors formerly committed by some of the extremists among the historical economists and not yet so infrequent as they ought to be. Obedience to law does not mean that the law causes the phenomenon to happen, — for that is absurd, — but simply that the law affords an explanation of the occurrence.

History, however, is the record of the actions of men in society. It is not alone past politics, as Freeman said, but past economics, and past ethics, and past jurisprudence, and past every other kind of social activity. But if each phase of social activity constitutes the material for a separate science, with its array of scientific laws, the whole of social activity, which in its ceaseless transformation forms the warp and woof of history, must equally be subject to law. All social activity may be regarded from the point of view of coexistence of phenomena or from that of sequence of phenomena. In the one case we arrive at the static laws, in the other at the dynamic laws. The laws of history are the dynamic laws of the social sciences or of the social science *par excellence*. To deny the existence of historical laws is to maintain that there is to be found in human life no such thing as cause and effect.

The third objection to the doctrine is its alleged socialistic character. To this it may be replied that, if the theory is true, it is utterly immaterial to what conclusion it leads. To refuse to accept a scientific law because some of its corollaries are distasteful to us is to betray a lamentable incapacity to grasp the elementary conditions of scientific progress. If the law is true, we must make our views conform to the law, not attempt to mould the law to our views.

Fortunately, however, we are not reduced to any such alternative. For, notwithstanding the ordinary opinion to the contrary, there is nothing in common between the economic interpretation of history and the doctrine of socialism, except the accidental fact that the originator of both theories happened to be the same man. Karl Marx founded "scientific socialism," if by that curious phrase we mean his theory of surplus value and the conclusions therefrom. Karl Marx also originated the economic interpretation of history and thought that his own version of this interpretation would prove to be a bulwark of his socialistic theory. And most of his followers have thought likewise. Thus, Mehring tells us that "historical idealism in its various theological, rationalistic and materialistic manifestations is the conception of history of the bourgeois class, as historical materialism is that of the laboring class."[1]

It is plain, however, that the two things have nothing to do with each other. We might agree that economic factors primarily influence progress; we might conclude that social forces, rather than individual whim, at bottom make history; we might perhaps even accept the existence of class struggles; but none of these admissions would necessarily lead to any semblance of socialism. Scientific socialism teaches that private property in capital is doomed to disappear; the economic interpretation of history calls attention, among other things, to the influence which private capital has exerted on progress. The vast majority of economic thinkers to-day believe, as a result of this historical study, that the principle of private property is a logical and salutary result of human development, however much they may be disposed to emphasize the need of social con-

[1] *Die Lessing-Legende*, p. 500.

trol. The Neo-Marxists themselves — such as Bernstein, for instance — disagree with Marx's view as to the immediate future of the class struggle, and consider that his doctrine of the "impending cataclysm of capitalistic society" has been disproved by the facts of the half century which has intervened since the theory was propounded. Yet Bernstein would not for a moment abandon his belief in the economic interpretation of history as we have described it.[1]

In fact, the socialistic application of the economic interpretation of history is exceedingly naïve. If history teaches anything at all, it is that the economic changes transform society by slow and gradual steps. It took centuries for feudal society to develop; it took centuries for private capital to convert feudalism into modern industrial society. The characteristic mark of the modern factory system, still in its infancy, is the predominance of the individual or corporate entrepreneur on a huge scale, as we see it typified in the present trust

[1] In his most recent book Bernstein speaks of the "realistische Geschichtsbetrachtung die in ihren Hauptzügen unwiderlegt geblieben ist." — *Zur Geschichte und Theorie des Sozialismus* (2d ed., 1901), p. 285.

movement in America. To suppose that private property and private initiative, which are the very secrets of the whole modern movement, will at once give way to the collective ownership which forms the ideal of the socialists, is to shut one's eyes to the significance of actual facts and to the teachings of history itself.[1] Rodbertus was at least more logical than Marx when he asserted that the triumph of socialism would be a matter of the dim future.

Socialism is a theory of what ought to be; historical materialism is a theory of what has been. The one is teleological, the other is descriptive. The one is a speculative ideal,[2] the other is a canon of interpretation. It is impossible to see any necessary connection between such divergent conceptions. Even if every one of Marx's economic theories was entirely false, this fact alone would not in any degree invalidate the general doctrine of economic interpretation. It is perfectly possible

[1] Marx, indeed, in one passage predicts the formation of trusts. But he, as well as his followers, overlooks the fact that concentrated capital, like separated capital, can do its best work only under the lash of individual initiative and personal responsibility.

[2] The "scientific socialists" deny this, but in vain.

to be the stanchest individualist and at the same time an ardent advocate of the doctrine of economic interpretation. In fact, the writers who are to-day making the most successful application of economic interpretation are not socialists at all. We might agree with the general doctrine and yet refuse to accept the somewhat fanciful ideals of the non-socialist Loria; we might agree with the general doctrine and yet refuse to accept the equally fanciful ideals of the socialist Marx. Socialism and "historical materialism" are at bottom entirely independent conceptions.

Furthermore, we must distinguish between the principle of economic interpretation in general, and some particular application of the principle. When the phrase "historical materialism" is mentioned in Germany, or in socialistic circles abroad, every one at once thinks of Karl Marx, because he has been virtually the only writer in Germany to attempt a consistent explanation of history on economic lines. "Historical materialism" and Marxism have thus come to be considered synonymous. In other countries, however, we find many different versions of the theory. To speak only of America, Gunton, Patten and Brooks Adams, who are by no means in thorough accord with each other, agree in ascribing the chief importance to economic factors. Yet each one of these writers would utterly refuse to be put in the same category as Marx.

We are not here concerned with the validity of some particular explanation of historical facts on economic lines. We are endeavoring to ascertain how far the theory of economic interpretation in general is tenable as a principle. To make the general principle stand or fall with some particular application would be narrow in the extreme. The problem of the truth of economic interpretation is not necessarily bound up with the Marxian version of such interpretation. Just as the Marxian economics must not be confused with economics in general, so the Marxian interpretation of history is by no means synonymous with economic interpretation in general.

But while socialism and "historical materialism" are thus in no way necessarily connected, it does not follow that they may not both be equally erroneous. All that we have attempted to prove here is that the falsity of socialism does not, of and in itself, connote the falsity of economic interpretation. The fact that one argument is bad does not imply that other arguments are good. The validity of the economic interpretation of history is still open to question and cannot be decided until after a study of other and far more important considerations.

NOTE TO SECOND EDITION.—Perhaps the ablest writer of the "revisionist" school of Socialists, Dr. Michael Tugan-Baranowsky, has abandoned one after another all of the claims of "scientific socialism." A large part of his recent book on *Theoretische Grundlagen des Marxismus*, 1905, is devoted to the economic interpretation of history. To the extent that Marx's "materialistic version of history" implies the existence of the class-struggle as the sole explanation of progress, Tugan-Baranowsky characterizes it as a fatal error (*grösster Irrtum*). He recognizes the fact, however, that this second doctrine (that of class-struggle) is not in any way a logical conclusion from the first doctrine (that the material economic factors are the determining elements in history). In other words, he confesses, what has been contended in the above pages, that the Marxist socialistic version of the economic interpretation of history is neither inevitable nor defensible. Tugan-Baranowsky then takes up in turn the labor theory of value, the doctrine of surplus-value, the impoverishment theory, and the doctrine of the cataclysm of society, showing that each one of these is no longer tenable in the face of the criticisms urged by the economists. What then, we may ask, is left of scientific socialism?

CHAPTER III

THE SPIRITUAL FACTORS IN HISTORY

THUS far we have set forth the theory of the economic interpretation of history and have studied some of the objections that are commonly advanced. There still remain among the criticisms most frequently encountered two points which seem to be somewhat more formidable. Of these perhaps the more important is the one that figured fourth in our original list,[1] — the objection, namely, that the theory of economic interpretation neglects the ethical and spiritual forces in history.

It must be confessed, indeed, that the attempts thus far made by the "historical materialists" to meet the objection have not been attended with much success.[2] On closer inspection, neverthe-

[1] *Supra*, p. 90.

[2] *Cf.* especially the controversy carried on between the Englishman Bax and the German Kautsky in *Die Neue Zeit*. For Bax, see vol. xv, pp. 175, 685; for Kautsky, see vol. xiv, p. 652, and vol. xv, pp. 231, 260. *Cf.* also Mehring, *Die Lessing-Legende*, p. 463; and the essay by Bernstein in *Die Neue Zeit*,

less, this criticism also turns out to be in some respects less weighty than has often been supposed.

For what, after all, is the realm of ethical or spiritual forces? To answer this question it is necessary to distinguish between the existence of the moral law and its genesis. The failure to draw this distinction is largely responsible for the confusion of thought which still prevails.

From the historical point of view it no longer admits of reasonable doubt that all individual ethics is the outgrowth of social forces. Moral actions are of two kinds, — those which directly affect other individuals, and those which primarily affect only one's self. In the first class, comprising to-day the great mass of activities to which we apply the term "ethical," the sanction was originally social in character. The conception of sin or immorality is not the primary conception. Historically we first find crimes and torts, that is, offences against society as a whole or against the individuals comprising

vol. xi, p. 782. Bernstein has also treated the subject in his more recent books.

As to the French socialists, see Labriola, *Essais sur la Conception Matérialiste de l'Histoire* (1897); Lafargue, *Idéalisme et Matérialisme* (1895); and Deville, *Principes Socialistes* (1896).

society; it is only at a much later period that the idea emerges of an offence against God or against the moral law as reflected in one's conscience. When the conception of sin was once reached, it was indeed gradually broadened so as to include the other offences, until to-day the commission of either crime or tort involves a sin. But historically sins were not recognized as such before torts and crimes.

Among brutes there is in all probability no such thing as morality, no conception of good or evil.[1] The female may protect her young through instinct; but to maintain that this is a moral action is, to say the least, premature. It no doubt conduces to the perpetuation of the species, and thus is a powerful factor in natural selection; but there is nothing moral about the action unless we are willing to apply the term "moral" to every act — whether instinc-

[1] The reason why it is not safe categorically to deny the existence of morality among animals is that the older contention of an essential psychical difference between man and animals has broken down before the flood of recent investigation. Comparative biology has proved that psychological phenomena begin far down in animal life. Some writers even profess to find them among the very lowest classes of beings — so low, indeed, that it is even doubtful whether they belong to the animal or the vegetable kingdom. For a popular presentation see Binet, *The Psychic Life of Micro-Organisms* (1894). Binet's views, however, are not shared by the more conservative biologists.

tive or volitional — that makes for the permanence of the species. Morality in its origin indeed implies utility; but utility does not necessarily connote morality. Even if we predicate morality of animals, however, future investigators will no doubt explain its origin on very much the same lines as that of human morality.

For with the institution of human society we are on safer ground and can trace the glimmerings of a moral development. In the primitive peoples that still exist in almost the lowest stages of savagery, the only offences that are recognized are even to-day offences against the horde or clan, that is, what we should call public offences or crimes. Treason, incest and witchcraft are the three great original crimes that are almost universally found. They are offences against the community, because they imperil, in the estimation of the people, the very existence of society. At first there is no idea of sin apart from these offences. The words "good" or "bad" are invariably applied only to actions affecting the social group. The very conception of wrong is a social conception. Certain actions come to be considered wrong because they are socially injurious. They are punished by society as a whole, and the cause of their punishment is to be found in the consciousness of society that they are infractions of the fundamental social customs which have been so laboriously developed. For these customs are the "teachings of mother nature drilled into countless generations of savage ancestors. They are lessons in social necessity, in social selection, where failure to learn or refusal to obey means the inevitable destruction of the social group — means social death."[1]

What has been said of crimes applies also to torts. The earliest offence of the aboriginal savage against his comrade carried with it no more moral implication than does to-day the killing of one animal by another. Passionate action and retaliation were originally with men, as they are still with brutes, the form assumed by the desire for physical mastery. The animal struggle for existence is neither moral nor immoral — it is unmoral. As soon, however, as the offence of man against man was taken notice of by society, as soon as the retaliation was regulated by social custom or law, the

[1] Hall, *Crime in its Relation to Social Progress. Columbia University Studies in History, Economics and Public Law*, XV (1902), p. 55

punishment was invested with a social sanction, and the act began to be regarded as reprehensible. When human beings came to see that certain actions directed against their fellows were followed by social reprobation or by individual vengeance resting on social approval, it did not take long to learn that if they valued their existence in society they must refrain from such actions. In the contest of man with man each individual always has a chance of victory; he therefore feels no certainty that a given act will be followed by any baneful consequences to him. But against a social group, the individual is powerless, and his opportunity for escape from punishment is slight.

In the course of ages social customs grow so rigid that any deviation from the habitual usage comes to be regarded not only as peculiar but as positively harmful, and therefore reprehensible. The fear of social disapproval and the hope of social approval become the forces which lead to the original ideas of evil or good as applied to the social actions of the individual.

Whether the conception of tort or that of crime is the earlier historically, need not be discussed here. Most writers assume that torts precede crimes; and it is undoubtedly true that many torts are gradually transformed into crimes. On the other hand, it is almost equally certain that some crimes have preceded torts. Adultery was a crime as incest before it was a tort; deception was a crime as treason before it was a tort. However that may be, the point of importance for us is that both torts and crimes are offences with a social sanction, and that before this social sanction existed there was no such idea as that of sin or immorality applicable to the actions of man to man.

The teachings of language itself afford a clear indication of the social origin of the conception of morality. The word "ethical" is derived from ἦθος, which means social custom or usage; just as "moral," which Cicero tells us[1] he coined in imitation of the Greek, is derived from *mos*, denoting precisely the same as ἦθος. So also the German term for moral, *sittlich*, is derived from *Sitte*, or social usage. It is society which has set the original imprint on the very conception of morality.

Not only is the idea of morality an historical product, but the content of morality changes

[1] Cicero, *De Fato*, cap. li.

with the state of civilization or with the social class. Homicide was at one time as little immoral as the killing of one animal by another is at present; it was simply unmoral. Even to-day it is not immoral if committed by a soldier in warfare; it becomes murder and sinful only when the same individual acts in some other capacity than that of a member of the army. Again, with reference to some acts it is not quite clear whether they are right or wrong. For instance, the deception practised by General Funston to entrap Aguinaldo is declared by some to be not wholly wrong because it scarcely, if at all, violated the social usages of civilized nations in warfare—provided, that is, that we are willing to confess that there is a difference between civilized and uncivilized warfare. On the other hand, the looting by some of the allies of the treasures in Pekin and Tien-tsin is conceded by almost every one to be wrong, because it has recently become a custom reprobated by the social conscience of the most civilized peoples.

Competition is still the rule in business life: economists call it neither moral nor immoral. But competition between members of the smaller social group known as the family is no longer deemed defensible, because it has long since been recognized by society at large that social welfare would, on the whole, be furthered by the practice of family coöperation. The taking of private property without compensation is ordinarily considered wrong; but when a man's house is blown up to check a conflagration, the action is neither morally nor legally wrong, because of the overmastering social considerations.

Thus the conception of right or wrong does not attach invariably to any particular action, because the same action may, under different circumstances and as applied to varying social stages, be both right and wrong. Since social considerations make the social actions of the individual right or wrong, the idea of good or evil itself is a social product.

What we have thus far said is true primarily of the social actions of individuals — of the acts of man to man. The principle, however, is equally applicable to the second class of moral actions referred to above — those, namely, which seem at first to affect the individual only. An individual, for instance, may be guilty of some particular practice upon himself, which we popularly declare to be not good for him, or a vice. Properly speaking, however, all that was originally meant was that it was not conducive to his physical or material welfare. Whiskey is not good for an ordinary child; whiskey is good for an invalid. In the original conception of good there is no idea of morality — of right or wrong. If an animal gorges itself to repletion, we do not ascribe any moral quality to the action. When the isolated savage first mutilated himself there was no thought of anything right or wrong, but only of what might be the physical or material consequences, irrespective of the fact whether these consequences might be brought out by natural forces or by the interposition of some supernatural spirit or demon.

Just as an individual called those things good which promoted his material welfare, so society called those things good which contributed to its continued existence. As soon as the idea of social advantage, however, forces itself through, we reach the conception of morality. An action is now reprobated or admired according as it conduces to the social welfare; and long-continued custom makes the individual conform his actions and ideas to this social standard, *i.e.*, creates in him the feeling of right or wrong.

Thus what is good physically for the individual becomes good morally only when the social test has been applied. Since this ethical connotation is the result of social forces, it is clear that acts which had originally only a physical significance for the individual gradually acquired an ethical significance because of the assumption that they would lead to certain social consequences. A member of modern society who will continually gorge himself will acquire certain characteristics that will make him distasteful to his fellow-men, or that will serve as a bad example to others. In either case it is the social considerations that attach an ethical significance to what is at bottom a mere individual physical act.

It is only when men have learned to live in society, and when they have come to fear that some individual practice will react upon their ideas or their actions in relation to other individuals, that they learn to attribute a moral quality even to acts which at first blush seem to bear no relation to any one else. The same is true of the actions of men toward animals. The killing of an animal as such is in itself neither good nor bad; but cruelty to animals is reprobated because of the probable effects on the character of the human being who commits the act. Thus all acts of the individual, whether they seem to affect himself alone or others, become good or bad only as the result of social considerations.

All individual morality is the outcome and the reflex of social morality.[1] Conscience itself,

[1] The theory of the social origin of morality has been brilliantly worked out by von Ihering in the second volume of his masterpiece *Der Zweck im Recht*, 1883 (2d ed., 1886). Von Ihering made no attempt to apply the theory to the general doctrine here under consideration. In English literature the earliest treatment of the subject is found in Darwin's *Descent of Man*, ch. iv. For an interesting adumbration of the theory of the social origin of morality, *cf.* the brilliant but very incomplete passages of W. K. Clifford in his articles "On the Scientific Basis of Morals" and "Right and Wrong," published originally in 1875 and reprinted in his *Lectures and Essays* II (1879), esp. pp. 111, 112, 114, 119–123, 169, 172–173. The admirable work of Alexander Sutherland, *The Origin and Growth of the Moral Instinct* (1898), bases the development of morality on the growth of sympathy through the family. Thus he tells us that "from the usages that grew up within the family sprung morality; from those that sprung up between the families grew law," II, p. 138; or again "true morality grows up within the family," II, p. 146; or again "moral rules as to bloodshed, honesty, truth, chastity are all, by birth, of family growth," II, p. 151. Sutherland forgets, however, that in early society it was not the family in the modern sense, but the horde, the clan and the tribe that formed the unitary social groups. Sutherland's book, nevertheless, is the first one in English clearly to point out that the (social) utilitarian theory of ethics has nothing "low" or "sordid" about it, but is really compatible with the most idealistic view of the universe. For the earlier and cruder opposition on the part of the intuitionists, see Miss Cobbe's "Darwinism in Morals," *Theological Review*, April, 1872, pp. 188–191.

or the ability to distinguish between good and bad, is the historical product of social forces. We must therefore agree with Sutherland when he defines the moral instinct as "that unconscious bias which is growing up in human minds in favor of those among our emotions that are conducive to social happiness."[1] We must equally subscribe to his statement that "there is no foundation of any sort for the view maintained by Kant and Green and Sidgwick, with so many others, that this inward sense (conscience) is innate — a supernatural, mysterious and unfailing judge of conduct. On the contrary, what society praises, the individual will in general learn to praise, and what he praises in others he will commend in himself."[2]

Whatever truth there may be in the intuitive or transcendental theory of ethics as a part of the cosmic scheme, there is no doubt that morality as applied to human beings is the result of a slow unfolding, in which social forces have played the chief rôle.

Such is the origin of the moral sense, whose existence and activity are undoubted facts of human life. It exerts a profound influence on

[1] *Op. cit.*, II, p. 306.

[2] *Ibid.*, II, p. 72.

the individual because it is the crystallization of centuries of social influences. So slow, however, has been the accumulating force of these influences that the individual is utterly oblivious of its social origin and importance. But, although conscience exists as a separate category, it does not lead an entirely independent life. It is like instinct with animals,—ages of dearly bought experience have served to put an almost indelible imprint on animal habits, until a certain course of action is followed instinctively.[1] The imprint, however, is not quite indelible. Just as the instinct is in its origin an historical product, it will inevitably be slowly moulded by future experiences. The instinct to preserve life remains; but the particular method, which is instinctively followed, changes from time to time. The instinct persists, but its form is modified. So the fact of moral con-

[1] This is not the place to discuss the various theories of instinct. A popular discussion may be found in Alfred Russell Wallace's *Darwinism*, p. 441, and a more technical one in Weissmann's *Essays on Heredity* and in C. L. Morgan's *Habit and Instinct*. It will suffice here to quote from Romanes: "There is ample evidence to show that instincts may arise either by natural selection fixing on purposeless habits which chance to be profitable, so converting these habits into instincts without intelligence being ever concerned in the process; or by habits, originally intelligent, becoming by repetition automatic."—*Mental Evolution in Animals*, p. 267.

sciousness in man and the existence of the ethical and spiritual life in civilized society are undoubted; but the content of this moral consciousness changes with the same forces that originally gave it birth.

It would, therefore, be absurd to deny that individual men, like masses of men, are moved by ethical considerations. On the contrary, all progress consists in the attempt to realize the unattainable,—the ideal, the morally perfect. History is full of examples where nations, like individuals, have acted unselfishly and have followed the generous promptings of the higher life. The ethical and the religious teachers have not worked in vain. To trace the influence of the spiritual life in individual and social development would be as easy as it is unnecessary. What is generally forgotten, however, and what it is needful to emphasize again and again, is not only that the content of the conception of morality is a social product, but also that amid the complex social influences that coöperated to produce it, the economic factors have often been of chief significance—that pure ethical or religious idealism has made itself felt only within the limitations of existing economic conditions.

The material, as we have seen, has almost always preceded the ethical. Individual actions, like social actions, possessed a material significance long before they acquired an ethical meaning. Etymology helps us here as it did in the discussion of the meaning of morality itself. A thing was originally a good in the material sense in which we still speak of "goods and commodities"; the ethical sense of good as opposed to bad came much later. In popular parlance we still speak of a broken nail as "no good" without desiring to pass any moral judgment on it. The original meaning of "dear" was not ethical, but economic; a commodity may still be "dear," even if we do not love it. To-day we esteem somebody; originally we put a money value on him (*æstimare* — from *æs*, money). In modern times we appreciate a quality; originally we set a price on it (*adpretium*). Everywhere the physical, material substratum was recognized long before the ethical connotation was reached.

Since the material precedes the ethical, it will not surprise us to learn that the material conditions of society — that is, in the widest sense, the economic conditions — continually modify the content of the ethical conception. Let us take a few illustrations at random. Slavery, for instance, was not considered wrong by the great Greek moralists, whose ethical views on many other topics were at least on a plane with those of modern times. In the same way the English colonists, who at home would have scouted the very idea of slavery, soon became in the southern states of America the most ardent and sincere advocates of the system; even the clergymen of the South honestly refused to consider slavery a sin. Had the northern and western states been subjected to the same climatic and economic conditions, there is little doubt that, so far at least as they could keep themselves shut off from contact with the more advanced industrial civilization of Europe, they would have completely shared the moral views of their southern brethren. Men are what conditions make them, and ethical ideals are not exempt from the same inexorable law of environment.

To the ethical teachers of the middle ages feudal rights did not seem to be wrongs. The hardy pioneers of New England needed a different set of virtues from those which their successors in a softer age have acquired; the attempt to subdue the Indian by love, charity and non-resistance would have meant not so much the disappearance of evil as the disappearance of the colonists. The moral ideal of a frontier society is as legitimate from the point of view of their needs as the very different ideal of a later stage of society. The virtue of hospitality is far more important in the pastoral stage than in the industrial. The ethical relation of master to workmen under the factory system is not the same as under the guild system. The idea of honor and of the necessity of duelling as a satisfaction for its violation is peculiar to an aristocratic or military class; with the change of economic conditions which make for democracy and industrialism, the content of the conception changes. We hear much of the growth of international law and of the application of ethical principles to international relations. We forget that such principles can come into existence only when the conditions are ripe. Universal peace can exist only when one country is so powerful that it dominates all the others, — as in the case of imperial Rome, — or when the chief nations have grown to be on such a footing of equality that none dares to offend its neighbor, and the minor countries are protected by the mutual jealousies of the great powers.

Political ethics are here precisely like private ethics. Individual vengeance does not disappear until all the citizens are subjected to the power of the strong tyrant, or until the people are willing to abide by the decision of the court, because of the conviction that before the law they are all equal. International law began when economic forces in the sixteenth and seventeenth centuries made the first step toward equality by converting the heterogeneous petty principalities into great nations; international justice and universal peace will come only when the economic changes now proceeding apace shall have converted the struggling nations of the present day into a few vast empires, dividing among themselves, and gradually civilizing, the outlying colonial possessions, thus attaining a condition of comparative economic equality. Economic equality among individuals creates the democratic virtues; economic equality among nations can alone prepare the way for international peace and justice.

Thus the economic interpretation of history, correctly understood, does not in the least seek to deny or to minimize the importance of ethical and spiritual forces in history. It only emphasizes the domain within which the ethical forces can at any particular time act with success. To sound the praises of mercy and love to a band of marauding savages would be futile; but when the old conditions of warfare are no longer really needed for self-defence, the moral teacher can do a great work in introducing more civilized practices, which shall be in harmony with the real needs of the new society. It is always on the border line of the transition from the old social necessity to the new social convenience that the ethical reformer makes his influence felt. With the perpetual change in human conditions there is always some kind of a border line, and thus always the need of the moral teacher, to point out the higher ideal and the path of progress. Unless the social conditions, however, are ripe for the change, the demand of the ethical reformer will be fruitless. Only if the conditions are ripe will the reform be effected.

The moral ideals are thus continually in the forefront of the contest for progress. The ethical teacher is the scout and the vanguard of society; but he will be followed only if he enjoys the confidence of the people, and the real battle will be fought by the main body of social forces, amid which the economic conditions are in last resort so often decisive. There is a moral growth in society, as well as in the individual. The more civilized the society, the more ethical its mode of life. But to become more civilized, to permit the moral ideals to percolate through continually lower strata of the population, we must have an economic basis to render it possible. With every improvement in the material condition of the great mass of the population there will be an opportunity for the unfolding of a higher moral life; but not until the economic conditions of society become far more ideal will the ethical development of the individual have a free field for limitless progress. Only then will it be possible to neglect the economic factor, which may thenceforward be considered as a constant; only then will the economic interpretation of history become a matter for archæologists rather than for historians.

Moral forces are, indeed, no less influential in human society than the legal and political forces. But just as the legal system, like the political system, conforms at bottom to the economic conditions, so the particular ethical system or code of morality has been at any given period very largely an outgrowth of the social, and especially of the economic, life. If by materialism we mean a negation of the power of spiritual forces in humanity, the economic interpretation of history is really not materialistic. But if by economic interpretation we mean — what alone we should mean — that the ethical forces themselves are essentially social in their origin and largely conditioned in their actual sphere of operation by the economic relations of society, there is no real antagonism between the economic and the ethical life.

The economic interpretation of history, in the reasonable and moderate sense of the term, does not for a moment subordinate the ethical life to the economic life; it does not even maintain that in any single individual there is a necessary connection between his moral impulses and his economic welfare; above all it does not deny an interpenetration of economic institutions by ethical or religious influences. It endeavors only to show that in the records of the past the moral uplift of humanity has been closely connected with its social and economic progress, and that the ethical ideals of the community, which can alone bring about any lasting advance in civilization, have been erected on, and rendered possible by, the solid foundation of material prosperity. In short, the economic conception of history, properly interpreted, does not neglect the spiritual forces in history; it seeks only to point out the terms on which the spiritual life has hitherto been able to find its fullest fruition.

CHAPTER IV

EXAGGERATIONS OF THE THEORY

We come now to the last count in the indictment that has usually been found against the theory of economic interpretation. It consists of the objection that the theory involves us in absurd exaggerations. In the way that it is commonly put, however, this objection, even if true, would be beside the mark.

It is indeed a fact that some of the enthusiastic advocates of economic interpretation have claimed too much, or have advanced explanations which are, for the present at least, not susceptible of proof. Thus the most brilliant of the Italian economists — Achille Loria — has published a number of books[1] in which he

[1] One of these has been translated by Professor Keasbey under the title: *The Economic Foundation of Society* (1899). The original Italian was published in 1885, and a third edition appeared in 1902 under the title *Le Basi Economiche della Costituzione Sociale*. His other important works bearing on the same general subject are *Analisi della Proprietà Capitalista* (1889), and his more recent works, *La Sociologia, il Suo Compito* (1901), and *Il Capitalismo e la Scienza* (1901).

has attempted to interpret a vast mass of historical phenomena from the economic point of view. Many of his statements are correct, and have been successfully defended against the attacks of his critics; but some of his explanations are obviously unsatisfactory. Above all he has laid too much stress upon the influence of land in modern society and has thus, in some cases, injured rather than aided the general theory of economic interpretation, of which only the particular application — even if an admirably suggestive one — is original with him.[1]

Other less brilliant writers have been guilty of even more extreme statements. Thus some have sought to make religion itself depend on economic forces. In this contention there is indeed a modicum of truth. We know that the religion of a pastoral people is necessarily different from that of an agricultural community. Marx himself pointed out that "the neces-

[1] It is a singular testimony to the neglect of Marx's writings outside of Germany that so many critics in England, France and Italy should have hailed Loria as the originator of the doctrine of economic interpretation. Even Professor Keasbey is not entirely free from this error. See the Translator's Preface (p. ix) to the English edition. Loria himself, however, has made no such claim. See his recent book, *Marx e la sua Dottrina* (1902), esp. cap. 31 "Intorno ad alcune Critiche dell' Engels."

sity for predicting the rise and fall of the Nile created Egyptian astronomy and with it the dominion of the priests as directors of agriculture."[1] A Russian scholar, starting from much the same conception, has shown that somewhat analogous conditions were responsible for the theocracies of the other Oriental nations.[2] Hence it may be granted that there is an undoubted economic element in the religions of the past, as well as in those of the present.[3] Perhaps the most striking attempt, however, to carry the theory beyond its legitimate bounds is that which has sought the explanation of Christianity itself in economic facts alone.[4] It

[1] *Capital* (English Translation), p. 523, note 1.

[2] Metschnikoff, *La Civilisation et les Grandes Fleuves Historiques*, 1889. Marx, who forestalled Metschnikoff in this respect, had said twenty years before: "One of the material bases of the power of the state over the small disconnected producing organisms in India was the regulation of the water supply." *Capital*, p. 523, note 2. Kautsky was led by this passage to study the conditions of the other Asiatic theocracies, and came to the same conclusion without knowing anything of Metschnikoff, whose book had appeared in the interval. See *Die Neue Zeit*, IX (1899), p. 447, note.

[3] Some of the social and economic aspects of modern religious movements have been emphasized by Thomas C. Hall, *The Social Meaning of the Modern Religious Movement in England* (1900).

[4] The economic interpretation of Christianity was first advanced by Kautsky in "Die Entstehung des Christenthums," *Die Neue Zeit*, III (1885), pp. 481 and 529, and by Engels in his

is indeed an accepted fact nowadays that much of the opposition to Jesus was due to his radical social programme and his alleged communistic views; it is equally certain that the economic conditions of the Roman Empire favored the reception of these new ideas. To contend, however, that Christianity was primarily an economic movement is to ignore the function of the spiritual forces which we have just been discussing.[1]

The theory of economic interpretation has been applied not only to religion but even to philosophy. The whole movement of thought, for instance, which we associate with the words Greek philosophy, has been explained in a ponderous volume as a phenomenon referable to essentially economic causes.[2] Eleutheropou-

essay on "Bruno Bauer und das Urchristenthum" in the *Züricher Sozialdemokrat* (1882), nos. 19, 20. It was developed by Engels in a subsequent article in *Die Neue Zeit*, in 1894, by E. H. Schmitt, also in *Die Neue Zeit*, XV (1897), i, p. 412, and by Kautsky in the chapter on "Der urchristliche Kommunismus" in the first volume of *Die Geschichte des Sozialismus* (1895).

[1] Some of the objections have been urged by Hermann, *Sozialistische Irrlehren von der Entstehung des Christentums*, 1899. Kohler, however, goes entirely too far in the other direction.

[2] This view was first advanced by Dr. Stillich in an article in *Die Neue Zeit*, XVI, 1, p. 580. This turned out, however, to be a plagiarism from the lectures of a Greek Privat-Docent, at Zürich, mentioned in the next note. See *Die Neue Zeit*, XVI, 2, p. 154.

los,[1] it is true, denies that he is attempting to prove the validity of historical materialism; for he claims to be a "philosopher" rather than a historical materialist, and he calls his theory the "Grecian theory of development."[2] On closer inspection, however, the difference between the two doctrines is scarcely discernible; for the author tells us that the "materialistic conception of history furnishes the key to the phenomenon of how the general character of philosophy as a *Weltanschauung* displays itself in different forms and shadings." He states indeed that more than this it cannot do, and that philosophy is also the product of the philosopher as an individual. "The theory of the economic relations of society as the cause of becoming can therefore be true only in the sense of the formal cause of development."[3] Yet in almost every section he attempts to trace the connection between the particular philosophic theory and the economic conditions. It is needless to say that the attempt is

[1] *Wirthschaft und Philosophie, oder die Philosophie und die Lebens-Auffassung der jeweils Bestehenden Gesellschaft. Erste Abtheilung: Die Philosophie und die Lebens-Auffassung des Griechentums auf Grund der Gesellschaftlichen Zustände.* Von Abr. Eleutheropoulos, 1898 (2d ed., 1900).

[2] Preface to second edition.

[3] *Op. cit.*, p. 16.

far from successful. The social philosophy of the Greeks is indeed an outcome of the social conditions, as is to be expected; but the search for the ultimate principles of life and thought, as we find it in the greatest of the Greek thinkers, has no conceivable relation with the actual economic conditions. The explanations of Eleutheropoulos are almost always far-fetched.

The economic interpretation of philosophy has not been confined to the Greek period. Another writer, presumably a socialist, has furnished an economic explanation of von Hartmann's philosophy, on the ground that the German *bourgeoisie* is giving up its class consciousness.[1] It is obviously not worth while to discuss this seriously.

Other more or less extreme applications of the theory are familiar to all. Among older writers that flourished before the theory itself was formulated, it will suffice to mention Alison, who ascribed the downfall of the Roman Empire to the monetary difficulties of the period, and those Spanish historians who made the decay of Spain turn upon the extension of the *alcavala* — the general tax on sales. To come to more recent authors, we need but

[1] Quoted in Masaryk, *Die Grundlagen des Marxismus*, p. 146.

mention Mr. Brooks Adams[1] and Professor Patten,[2] who, amid much that is suggestive, have centred their attention upon particular economic conditions in the history of Rome and England respectively, and have ascribed to these an influence on general national development out of all proportion to their real significance.

Such invalid applications of the theory, however, do not necessarily invalidate the doctrine itself. We must distinguish here, as in every other domain of human inquiry, between the use and the abuse of a principle. The difference between the scientist and the fanatic is that the one sees the limitations of a principle, where the other recognizes none. To make any science or any theory responsible for all the vagaries of its over-enthusiastic advocates would soon result in a discrediting of science itself. Wise men do not judge a race by its least fortunate members; fair-minded critics do not estimate the value of a doctrine by its excrescences.

It is, however, important to remember that the originators of the theory have themselves called attention to the danger of exaggeration. Toward the close of his career Engels, influ-

[1] *The Law of Civilisation and Decay.*

[2] *The Development of English Thought.*

enced no doubt by the weight of adverse criticism, pointed out that too much had sometimes been claimed for the doctrine. "Marx and I," he writes to a student in 1890, "are partly responsible for the fact that the younger men have sometimes laid more stress on the economic side than it deserves. In meeting the attacks of our opponents it was necessary for us to emphasize the dominant principle, denied by them; and we did not always have the time, place or opportunity to let the other factors, which were concerned in the mutual action and reaction, get their deserts."[1] In another letter Engels explains his meaning more clearly:—

"According to the materialistic view of history the factor which is *in last instance* decisive in history is the production and reproduction of actual life. More than this neither Marx nor I have ever asserted. But when any one distorts this so as to read that the economic factor is the sole element, he converts the statement into a meaningless, abstract, absurd phrase. The economic condition is the basis, but the

[1] This letter is printed in *Der Sozialistische Akademiker*, October 1, 1895, and is quoted by Greulich, *Ueber die Materialistische Geschichts-Auffassung* (1897), p. 7, and by Masaryk, *Die Grundlagen des Marxismus* (1899), p. 104.

various elements of the superstructure — the political forms of the class contests, and their results, the constitutions — the legal forms, and also all the reflexes of these actual contests in the brains of the participants, the political, legal, philosophical theories, the religious views . . . — all these exert an influence on the development of the historical struggles, and in many instances determine their form."[1]

[1] "Nach materialistischer Geschichts-auffassung ist das in letzter Instanz bestimmende Moment in der Geschichte die Produktion und Reproduktion des wirklichen Lebens. Mehr hat weder Marx noch Ich je behauptet. Wenn nun jemand das dahin verdreht, das ökonomische Moment sei das einzig bestimmende, so verwandelt er jenen Satz in eine nichtssagende, abstrakte, absurde Phrase. Die ökonomische Lage ist die Basis, aber die verschiedenen Momente des Ueberbaues — politische Formen des Klassenkampfes und seine Resultate — Verfassungen, nach gewonnener Schlacht durch die siegende Klasse festgestellt, u. s. w. — Rechtsformen, und nun gar die Reflexe aller dieser wirklichen Kämpfe im Gehirn der Beteiligten, politische, juristische, philosophische Theorien, religiöse Anschauungen und deren Weiterentwicklung zu Dogmensystemen, üben auch ihre Einwirkung auf den Verlauf der geschichtlichen Kämpfe aus und bestimmen in vielen Fällen vorwiegend deren Form. Es ist eine Wechselwirkung aller dieser Momente, worin schliesslich durch alle die unendliche Menge von Zufälligkeiten (d. h. von Dingen und Ereignissen, deren innerer Zusammenhang untereinander so entfernt oder so unnachweisbar ist, dass wir ihn als nicht vorhanden betrachten, vernachlässigen können) als Notwendigkeit die ökonomische Bewegung sich durchsetzt. Sonst wäre die Anwendung der Theorie auf eine beliebige Geschichtsperiode ja leichter als die Lösung einer einfachen Gleichung ersten Grades." *Der Sozialistische Akademiker* (October 15, 1895), p. 351. Re-

To ascribe everything to economic changes is plainly inadmissible. Engels himself pointed out in another place that to attempt to explain every fact of history on economic grounds is not only pedantic but ridiculous.[1] Political conditions and national traditions much more often play an important rôle. To say, for instance, that Brandenburg of all the German states should have been selected to become the great power of the future solely because of eco-

printed in Woltmann, *Der Historische Materialismus* (1900), p. 239. *Cf.* also Engels' view of the importance of idealistic elements in a second letter of 1890 printed in the *Leipziger Volkszeitung* (1895), no. 250 (reprinted in Woltmann, p. 243), and in a further letter of 1893 printed in the second edition of F. Mehring's *Geschichte der Deutschen Sozialdemokratie*, Zweiter Theil, p. 556.

[1] "Es wird sich kaum ohne Pedanterie behaupten lassen, dass unter den vielen Kleinstaaten Norddeutschlands gerade Brandenburg durch ökonomische Notwendigkeit und nicht auch durch andere Momente (vor allen seine Verwicklung, durch den Besitz von Preussen, mit Polen und dadurch mit internationalen politischen Verhältnissen — die ja auch bei der Bildung der östreichischen Hausmacht entscheidend sind) dazu bestimmt war, die Grossmacht zu werden, in der sich der ökonomische, sprachliche und seit der Reformation auch religiöse Unterschied des Nordens vom Südem verkörperte. Es wird schwerlich gelingen, die Existenz jedes deutschen Kleinstaates der Vergangenheit und Gegenwart oder den Ursprung der hochdeutschen Lautverschiebung, die die geographische, durch die Gebirge von den Sudeten bis zum Taunus gebildete, Scheidewand zu einem förmlichen Riss durch Deutschland erweiterte, ökonomisch zu erklären, ohne sich lächerlich zu machen." — *Der Sozialistische Akademiker*, *loc. cit.*

nomic considerations, is foolish. To claim that every petty German principality was destined to live or to die for economic reasons alone, would be as absurd as to ascribe the difference between the various German dialects solely to economic causes.

Thus we see the doctrine of "historical materialism" in its crude form repudiated even by its founders. And it is unfortunately true that many "historical materialists," by the very exaggeration and vehemence of their statements, have brought discredit on a doctrine which, in a sublimated form, contains so large an element of truth and which has done so much for the progress of science.

CHAPTER V

TRUTH OR FALSITY OF THE THEORY

WHAT then shall we say of the doctrine of economic interpretation?

That its authors originally claimed too much for it, or at least framed the doctrine so as to give rise to misconception, is undoubtedly true. That some of its advocates have gone entirely too far is equally sure. And it is above all certain that the choice of the term "historical materialism" is unfortunate. The materialistic view of history, like the utilitarian theory of morals, has had to suffer more because of its name than because of its essence. The one is as little sordid as the other.

The economic interpretation of history, correctly understood, does not claim that every phenomenon of human life in general, or of social life in particular, is to be explained on economic grounds. Few writers would trace the different manifestations of language or even of art primarily to economic conditions;

still fewer would maintain that the various forms of pure science have more than a remote connection with social conditions in general. Man is what he is because of mental evolution, and even his physical wants are largely transformed and transmuted in the crucible of reasoning. The facts of mentality must be reckoned with.

It is an error,[1] however, to suppose that the theory of economic interpretation can be set aside by refuting the supposed claim that the economic life is genetically antecedent to the social or the mental life. The theory makes no such claim.

The whole contention as to the precedence in time of an assumed cause over a given effect is quite beside the mark. It reminds one of the old query as to which came first — the egg or the chicken. There is no longer any dispute among biologists as to the influence of environment. When, however, we speak of the transformation of a given species, we do not necessarily mean that the environment was

[1] Committed, for instance, by my honored colleague, Professor Giddings, in his interesting article, "The Economic Ages," *Political Science Quarterly* (June, 1901). Almost the same argument was made by Salvadori, *La Scienza Economica e la Teoria dell' Evoluzione* (1901), pp. 58–63.

there first, and that the organism came later. Without the environment there can indeed be no change; but without the organism there can also be no change. The adaptation of the organism to the environment simply means that those among the existing variations are selected which conduce most to the perpetuation of the species. If there were no existing variations or sports there would be no transformation. The fact that the variation may have existed before the change in environment occurs is no objection to the theory of adjustment of the organism to the environment. Although we say that the organism is determined by the environment, it is quite immaterial which existed first.

So it is with humanity. All human progress is at bottom mental progress; all changes must go through the human mind. There is thus an undoubted psychological basis for all human evolution. The question, however, still remains: What determines the thought of humanity? Even if we say that the answer is to be sought in the social conditions, the statement is irrespective of the genetic antecedence of the social environment to the mental life. It is quite true that the kernel of Marx's whole doctrine is to be found in the celebrated sentence: "It is not the consciousness of mankind that determines its existence, but on the contrary its social existence that determines its consciousness."[1] However extreme this statement may be on its purely philosophical side, it is not open to one criticism so frequently advanced; it does not necessarily imply that the social existence comes first, and the consciousness afterwards. Such an implication is as unwarranted as it would be in the analogous doctrine of biology; when biologists tell us that the organism is determined by the environment they do not necessarily make any hypothesis as to the priority of the one to the other. The whole question of genetic antecedence is unimportant.

Of far more significance, however, is the criticism based on the alleged insufficiency of the economic factor to explain the changes in social life in general. There is little doubt that the extreme advocates of "historical materialism" have laid themselves open to attack

[1] "Es ist nicht das Bewusstsein der Menschen, das ihr Sein, sondern ihr gesellschaftliches Sein, das ihr Bewusstsein bestimmt." —Marx, *Zur Kritik der Politischen Oekonomie*, Vorwort, p. v. The whole controversy of Hollitscher, *Das Historische Gesetz* (1901), pp. 93 *et seq.*, misses the real point.

from philosophers and historians alike. They have sometimes seemed to claim that all sociology must be based exclusively on economics, and that all social life is nothing but a reflex of the economic life.[1] No such claim, however, can be countenanced, and no such claim is made by the moderate advocates of the theory.

The claim cannot be countenanced for the obvious reason that economics deals with only one kind of social relations, and that there are as many kinds of social relations as there are classes of social wants. We have not only economic wants, but also moral, religious, jural, political and many other kinds of collective wants; we have not only collective wants, but individual wants, like physical, technical, æsthetic, scientific, philosophical wants. The term "utility," which has been appropriated by the economist, is not by any means peculiar to him. Objects may have not only an economic utility, but a physical, æsthetic, scientific, technical, moral, religious, jural, political or philosophical utility. The value which is the expression of this utility and which forms the

[1] Among these extremists must be classed Loria, who has advanced his views most clearly in his interesting work *La Sociologia*. In this he seeks to distinguish an economic sociology from the biologic or psychologic sociology of other writers.

subject-matter of economics is only one subdivision of a far greater class. For all the world is continually rating objects and ideas according to their æsthetic, scientific, technical, moral, religious, jural, political or philosophical value, without giving any thought to their economic value. So far as utility and value are social in character, that is, so far as they depend upon the relation of man to man, they form the subject-matter of sociology. Economics deals with only one kind of social utilities or values and can therefore not explain all kinds of social utilities or values. The strands of human life are manifold and complex.[1]

[1] An interesting criticism of "historical materialism" from this point of view and with especial reference to the influence of economics on law is made by Rudolf Stammler, Professor of Law in Halle, in his rather ponderous work, *Wirthschaft und Recht nach der Materialistischen Geschichtsauffassung* (1896). Stammler is far fairer to Marx than most of the opponents of the theory. He considers the attempt of Marx as in many ways a most remarkable one and deserving of high praise; but he nevertheless objects to the theory as unfinished and not completely thought out. Stammler does not contend that no monistic explanation of social life is possible. In fact his own synthesis is constructed on teleological lines — an explanation which regards all past social life in the light of social purposes or a social ideal. With special reference to the relation between law and economics, he defines social life as a "common activity regulated from without" (ein äusserlich geregeltes Zusammenwirken), and maintains that these external rules govern at once the legal, political, economic and other social relations. It is un-

In this aspect, what is untrue of the individual cannot be true of the group of individuals. We have passed beyond the time when it was incumbent to explain the fallacy lurking in the phrase "the economic man." There is indeed an economic life and an economic motive—the motive which leads every human being to satisfy his wants with the least outlay of effort. But it is no longer necessary to show that the individual is impelled by other motives than the economic one, and that the economic motive itself is not everywhere equally strong, or equally free from the admixture of other influences. A full analysis of all the motives that influence men, even in their economic life, would test the powers of the social psychologist. There is no "economic man," just as there is no "theological man." The merchant has family ties just as the clergyman has an appetite.

The wealth which forms the subject-matter of economic activity can be increased only through the multiplication of commodities; but this multiplication can take place only in

philosophical, then, so he tells us, to claim that any one set of social relations is the general cause or explanation of other social relations. They are all the common product of the same cause.

connection with an increased demand. Increased demand, however, means a diversification of wants. The things wanted by an individual depend in last resort on his æsthetic, intellectual and moral condition. The economic life is thus ultimately bound up with the whole ethical and social life. Deeper than is often recognized is the meaning of Ruskin's statement, "There is no wealth but life," and of his further claim, "Nor can any noble thing be wealth except to a noble person." The goal of all economic development is to make wealth abundant and men able to use wealth correctly.

If society, then, is an aggregation of individuals, and if history is the record of the activities of the social group and its constituent elements, history is the parti-colored garb of humanity.

In one sense, accordingly, there are as many methods of interpreting history as there are classes of human activities or wants. There is not only an economic interpretation of history, but an ethical, an æsthetic, a political, a jural, a linguistic, a religious and a scientific interpretation of history. Every scholar can thus legitimately regard past events from his own particular standpoint.

Nevertheless, if we take a broad view of human development, there is still some justification for speaking of *the* economic interpretation of history as the important one, rather than of *an* economic interpretation among other equally valid explanations. The broad reasons which lead to this conclusion may be summed up as follows.

Human life has thus far not been exempt from the inexorable law of nature, with its struggle for existence through natural selection. This struggle has assumed three forms. We find first the original struggle of group with group, which in modern times has become the contest of people with people, of nation with nation. Secondly, with the differentiation of population there came the rivalry of class with class: first, of the sacerdotal with the military and the industrial class; later, of the moneyed interest with the landed interest; still later, of the labor class with one or all of the capitalist classes. Thirdly, we find within each class the competition of the individuals to gain the mastery in the class. These three forms of conflict are in last resort all due to the pressure of life upon the means of subsistence; individual competition, class competition and race competition are all referable to the niggardliness of nature, to the inequality of human gifts, to the difference in social opportunity. Civilization indeed consists in the attempt to minimize the evils, while conserving the benefits of this hitherto inevitable conflict between material resources and human desires. As long, however, as this conflict endures, the primary explanation of human life must continue to be the economic explanation — the explanation of the adjustment of material resources to human desires. This adjustment may be modified by æsthetic, religious and moral, in short, by intellectual and spiritual forces; but in last resort it still remains an adjustment of life to the wherewithal of life.

When a more ideal economic adjustment is finally reached — that is, when science shall have given us a complete mastery over means of production, when the growth of population shall be held in check by the purposive activity of the social group, when progress in the individual and the race shall be possible without any conflict except one for unselfish ends, and when the mass of the people shall live as do to-day its noblest members — then, indeed, the economic conditions will fall into the background and will be completely overshadowed by the other social factors of progress. But until that period is reached, the economic conditions of the social group and of the mass of individuals must continue to retain their ascendency.

From the beginning of social life up to the present the rise, the progress and the decay of nations have been largely due to changes in the economic relations, internal and external, of the social groups, even though the facility with which mankind has availed itself of this economic environment has been the product of intellectual and moral forces. While the study of the economic factors alone will manifestly not suffice to enable us to explain all the myriad forms in which the human spirit has clothed itself since history began, it is none the less true that so long as the body is not everywhere held in complete subjection to the soul, so long as the struggle for wealth does not everywhere give way to the struggle for virtue, the social structure and the fundamental relations between social classes will be largely shaped by these overmastering influences, which, whether we approve or deplore them, still form so great a part of the content of life.

Human activity is indeed the activity of sentient beings, and, therefore, the history of mankind is the history of mental development; but human life depends upon the relation between the individual and his environment. In the struggle that has thus far gone on between individuals and groups in their desire to make the best of their environment, the paramount considerations have necessarily been economic in character. The view of history which lays stress on these paramount considerations is what we call the economic interpretation of history. They are not the exclusive considerations, and in particular instances the action and reaction of social forces may give the decisive influence to non-economic factors. Taking man, however, for what he has thus far been and still is, it is difficult to deny that the underlying influence in its broadest aspects has very generally been of this economic character. The economic interpretation of history, in its proper formulation, does not exhaust the possibilities of life and progress; it does not explain all the niceties of human development; but it emphasizes the forces which have hitherto been so largely instrumental in the rise and fall, in the prosperity and decadence, in the glory and failure, in the weal and woe of nations and peoples. It is a relative, rather than an absolute, explanation. It is substantially true of the past; it will tend to become less and less true of the future.

CHAPTER VI

FINAL ESTIMATE OF THE THEORY

If we ask, in conclusion, what importance shall be assigned to the theory of economic interpretation, we must consider it from two different points of view.

From the purely philosophical standpoint, it may be confessed that the theory, especially in its extreme form, is no longer tenable as the universal explanation of all human life. No monistic interpretation of humanity is possible, or, at all events, none will be possible until that most difficult of all studies — sociology — succeeds in finally elaborating the laws of its existence and thus vindicating its claim to be a real science. As a philosophical doctrine of universal validity, the theory of "historical materialism" can no longer be successfully defended.

But in the narrower sense of economic interpretation of history — in the sense, namely, that the economic factor has been of the utmost importance in history, and that the historical factor must be reckoned with in economics—the theory has been, and still is, of considerable significance. What is this significance to economics as well as to history?

In economics the old controversy as to the respective merits of the deductive and the inductive methods has been laid to rest. It is now recognized that both methods are legitimate and even necessary. The older antagonism to the quest for natural law in economics is now seen to be due to a confusion of thought and to a mistaken identification of natural law with immutable precepts. When the earlier writers spoke of the law of free trade, or of the inexorable law of *laissez faire*, they did not use the term "law" in the sense of scientific law, or a statement of the necessary relations between facts. Yet this is the only sense in which the term is properly employed. The removal of the older teleological connotation has left the conception of natural law in economics as innocent and as valuable as it is in any so-called pure science. While the explanation of what actually exists, however, forms an undoubted part of all science, the study of how these things have come to be what they are is perhaps of more importance in the social disciplines than in all others. The realization of the fact that social institutions are products of evolution, and that they thus form historical and relative categories, instead of being absolute categories, is the one great acquisition of modern economics, which differentiates it *toto cælo* from that of earlier times.

The acceptance of the principle of growth and of historic relativity is due to several causes. The historical school of jurisprudence in Germany, under Savigny and Eichhorn, did much to prepare men's minds for the reception of what now seems an obvious truth in legal science. The historical school of economists, under Roscher, Hildebrand and Knies, did more to familiarize the public with the newer conception. The influence of Darwin and the application of Darwinian methods to social science by Spencer and Wallace did still more to reënforce the idea of growth by the doctrines of evolution and natural selection. The jurisconsults, however, confined themselves to law, the historical economists, at the beginning at least, did not realize the connection between the economic and the wider social life, and the Darwinians came on the scene at a later date. Comte, indeed, influenced no doubt by Saint-Simon, had called attention to the relation between economics and sociology, but his own fund of economic knowledge was exceedingly slight. Long before Spencer wrote, Karl Marx, in a way undreamt of by the historical economists and unrecognized by Comte, not only stated that every economic institution is an historical category, but pointed out in a novel and fruitful way the connection between economic and social facts.

It is always hazardous to ascribe a complex change of thought to simple causes, and there is no doubt that the newer stream of economic thought is due to various currents of influence; but it is safe to predict that when the future historian of economics and social science comes to deal with the great transition of recent years, he will be compelled to assign to Karl Marx a far more prominent place than has hitherto been customary outside of the narrow ranks of the socialists themselves. In pure economic theory the work of Karl Marx, although brilliant and subtle, will probably live only because of its critical character; but in economic method and in social philosophy, Marx will long be remembered as one of those great pioneers who, even if they are not able themselves to reach the goal, nevertheless blaze out a new and promising path in the wilderness of human thought and human progress. The economic interpretation of history, in emphasizing the historical basis of economic institutions, has done much for economics.

On the other hand, it has done even more for history. It has taught us to search below the surface. The great-man theory of history, which was once so prevalent, simplified the problem to such an extent that history was in danger of becoming a mere catalogue of dates and events. The investigation of political and diplomatic relations indeed somewhat broadened the discipline and for a long time occupied the energies of the foremost writers. The next step in advance was taken when, under the influence of the school of historical jurisprudence, more attention was paid to the relations of public law, and when political progress was shown to rest largely on the basis of constitutional history. The study of the development of political institutions gradually replaced that of the mere record of political events. Legitimate and indispensable as was this step, it did not go far enough. Those writers, still so numerous, who understand by history primarily constitutional history, show that they only half comprehend the condition and the spirit of modern historical science.

The newer spirit in history emphasizes not so much the constitutional as the institutional side in development, and understands by institutions, not merely the political institutions, but the wider social institutions of which the political form only one manifestation. The emphasis is now put upon social growth, and national as well as international life is coming more and more to be recognized as the result of the play and interplay of social forces. It is for this reason that history is nowadays at once far more fascinating and immeasurably more complicated than was formerly the case. History now seeks to gauge the influence of factors some of which turn out to be exceedingly elusive. It attempts to introduce into the past the outlines of a social science whose very principles have not yet been adequately and permanently elaborated.

Whatever be the difficulties of the task, however, the new ideal is now more and more clearly recognized. In the formulation of this new ideal the theory of economic interpretation has played an important, if not always a consciously recognized, rôle. It is not that the historian of the future is to be simply an economic historian, for the economic life does not constitute the whole of social life. It is, however, the theory of economic interpretation that was largely responsible for turning men's minds to the consideration of the social factor in history. Marx and his followers first emphasized in a brilliant and striking way the relation of certain legal, political and constitutional facts to economic changes, and first attempted to present a unitary conception of history. Even though it may be conceded that this unitary conception is premature, and even if it is practically certain that Marx's own version of it is exaggerated, if not misleading, it is scarcely open to doubt that through it in large measure the ideas of historians were directed to some of the momentous factors in human progress which had hitherto escaped their attention. Regarded from this point of view the theory of economic interpretation acquires an increased significance. Whether or not we are prepared to accept it as an adequate explanation of human progress in general, we must all recognize the beneficent influence that it has exerted in stimulating the thoughts of scholars and in broadening the concepts and the ideals of history and economics alike. If for no other reason, it will deserve well of future investigators and will occupy an honored place in the record of mental development and scientific progress.

Printed in Dunstable, United Kingdom

91220743R00100